DEAD LINES

Essays in Murder and Mayhem

JACK LEVIN

Northeastern University

JAMES ALAN FOX

Northeastern University

ALLYN AND BACON

Boston ■ London ■ Toronto ■ Sydney ■ Tokyo ■ Singapore

*To Shelly Cohen, Marjorie Pritchard, and the other newspaper editors
who have helped to get our opinions into print*

Editor in Chief, Social Sciences: *Karen Hanson*
Editorial Assistant: *Sarah McGaughey*
Marketing Manager: *Jude Hall*
Editorial Production Service: *Marbern House*
Manufacturing Buyer: *Megan Cochran*
Cover Administrator: *Brian Gogolin*
Electronic Composition: *Omegatype Typography, Inc.*

Internet: www.abacon.com

ISBN: 0-205-33521-7

Printed in the United States of America

10   9   8   7   6   5   4   3   2   1   05   04   03   02   01   00

CONTENTS

Colleges and universities are frequently regarded disparagingly as "Ivory Towers," in which professors publish their research findings in arcane journals and write obscure monographs that have no relevance to the real world. The image is replete with stereotypes depicting the academic as lacking in any serious concern for applying research to real-life problems confronting average citizens.

The field of criminology certainly belies the myth of the detached academic. Of course, there are some criminologists who prefer to maintain their distance from popular culture and public policy. But there are many more who have testified before Congress and other legislative bodies, served as advisors to presidents, governors and mayors, lobbied for and against certain legislation, acted as expert witnesses, and written policy recommendations and critiques.

Virtually all the 52 essays in this volume were originally printed as opinion columns in newspapers around the country. They reflect our own desire to influence public opinion and public policy concerning efforts at reducing violent crime.

Our essays on murder and mayhem have been organized into the following sections: murder rate trends, juvenile homicide, school shootings, rampages, hate homicides, serial murder, murder and popular culture, the criminal justice system response, the death penalty, and victim issues. In each section, we focus our attention not only on the circumstances and motivations for murder, but also on solutions. In many essays, we suggest answers; in others, we ask questions and are critical of the answers proposed and implemented by policy makers.

Most of the essays in this volume were published during the last several years. A few were written as long ago as the 1980s, but are relevant to contemporary issues. For the most part, we have left them unchanged so as not to destroy their arguments. Finally, we introduce each essay bibliographically as well as contextually with its source and purpose.

We want to acknowledge and thank many people who in some important respects have helped us complete this project. Arnold Arluke, Jennifer Balboni, Heather Johnson, and Jack McDevitt have co-authored some of the columns in their original versions, and we appreciate their contributions. Our editor Karen Hanson of Allyn and Bacon gave us the encouragement and support that we needed in this project as in others. Finally, we are indebted to op-ed editors around the country who give academics an opportunity to reach an audience of millions.

Jack Levin
James Alan Fox

ABOUT THE AUTHORS

Jack Levin is the Irving and Betty Brudnick Professor of Sociology and Criminology and James Alan Fox is the Lipman Family Professor of Criminal Justice, both at Northeastern University in Boston. Among their numerous books, Fox and Levin have collaborated on four previous volumes related to murder, *Mass Murder: America's Growing Menace, Overkill: Mass Murder and Serial Killing Exposed, Killer on Campus,* and their latest, *The Will to Kill: Making Sense of Senseless Murder* (Allyn & Bacon, 2000). Independently or collaboratively, they have published over one hundred op-ed columns in newspapers around the country, including the *Boston Globe, Boston Herald, Chicago Tribune, Dallas Morning News, Los Angeles Times, New York Times, Philadelphia Inquirer,* and *USA Today.* As nationally recognized authorities on homicide, they appear often on national television programs, are frequently quoted in the national press, and have testified in various legislative hearings and criminal trials. They also lecture widely on topics related to violent crime in America.

PART I

HOMICIDE TRENDS

The Crime Generation Grows Up Right on Schedule

In this essay published in USA Today *(March 6, 1985), James Alan Fox speculated about a future crime wave based on demographics. This hypothesis concerning the link between population changes and crime trends later received attention when crime rates actually began to rise.*

In 1981, I testified before the House Subcommittee on Crime that the crime rate in America, and particularly violent crime, would decline, beginning with the 1981 figures and continuing for the remainder of the decade.

Although based on statistical projections constructed in my 1978 book, *Forecasting Crime Data*, my optimistic prediction was met with skepticism. After all, the sun rises every morning and crime goes up every year—or so it seemed.

The rate of crime has indeed dropped each year since 1981. The demographic explanation is, by this time, fairly well known: Crime is declining because the adolescent population—those with a greater propensity toward committing street crime—is now shrinking in proportionate size.

Despite its logical appeal, the demographic argument is not widely embraced, particularly by politicians, police chiefs, and legislators who understandably would much rather credit successful police strategies and stiffer sentencing laws for reductions in their local crime rates. The greater plausibility of the demographic argument, however, goes beyond the fact that it predicted recent crime trends long before they occurred. It is only demographics that can explain why the crime rate is falling, almost uniformly across the USA, in states and cities whose laws. policies, and practices are hardly uniform or even similar.

One shouldn't criticize the politicians and the police too harshly for taking the credit. They took the blame during the crime explosion of the 1960s, when few understood the impact on crime of an expanding adolescent population.

I do not suggest that local efforts to curb crime have been without merit, only that their presumed benefits in terms of crime reduction must be measured against that which was expected—and predicted—to happen regardless.

I encourage local efforts in crime prevention. We may become complacent thinking we have the crime problem licked as the crime rate continues its downward trend.

But in the 1990s, there will be another crime wave—smaller than the previous—as a consequence of the "baby-boomerang effect." The adolescent population will again swell with the offspring of the baby-boom generation.

When this happens it will be interesting to see where blame is cast. Will we focus on the diminishing role of the family, on economic recession, on drug abuse, on a criminal justice system that is perceived to be soft on criminals? Or will we remember the lesson in demography that we have learned in the past 20 years?

The Calm before the Crime Wave Storm

This essay written by James Alan Fox for the Los Angeles Times *(October 30, 1995) further develops the demographic argument. It suggests that in the overall crime picture, we must not overlook trends in youth crime.*

Despite the steady stream of bleak headlines about teens murdering one another over things like bad jokes or leather jackets, there actually has been some good news on the crime front. The National Center for Health Statistics announced its preliminary tabulations for 1994, which revealed that the homicide rate in America dropped 8 percent, extending a downward trend since 1991. And well into 1995, several major cities, including New York, Houston, Chicago, Detroit, and Los Angeles, are already boasting of substantial drops this year in their homicide counts.

Aided by federal funding, police chiefs around the country are beginning to feel that they can make some headway in combating the plague of street crime. The spread of community policing—putting more cops on the street to fight crime and disorder in a proactive way—has clearly revolutionized law enforcement much for the better. At the same time, Congress has passed the Brady bill as well as a ban on assault rifles. More cops on the streets and more caps on gun sales have translated into less crime.

Though these trends are encouraging, at least superficially, there is little time to celebrate. It is doubtful that today's improving crime picture will last very long. This may be the calm before the crime storm. Hidden in the overall drop in homicide and other violent crimes is a soaring rate of mayhem among teenagers.

There are actually two crime trends in America—one for the young, one for the mature—which are moving in opposite directions and balancing off in the statistics. For example, from 1990 to 1993 (the last year for which detailed national data are available), the rate of murder in America remained virtually unchanged—9.5 per 100,000 of population. While the murder rate committed by adults 25 and older fell 10 percent, the rate among young adults 18 to 24 rose 14 percent and for teenagers jumped a whopping and tragic 26 percent.

3

The surge in youth violence has occurred while the population in the prime crime age group—teens and young adults—was on the decline. But this demographic benefit is about to change.

As a consequence of the "baby boomerang" (the offspring of the baby boomers), there are now 39 million children in this country under 10, more young children than we've had for decades. Millions of them live in poverty. Most do not have full-time parental supervision at home guiding their development and supervising their behavior. Of course, these children will not remain young for long; they will reach their high-risk years before you can say "juvenile crime wave."

By the year 2005, the number of teens ages 14 to 17 will swell by 14 percent, with an even larger increase among people of color—17 percent among black teens and 30 percent among Latino teens. Given the difficult conditions in which many of these youngsters grow up—with inferior schools and violence-torn neighborhoods—many more teenagers will be at risk in the years ahead.

The challenge is how best to deal with youth violence. The good news is that we now have some of the tools with which to deal effectively with the problem of teens, guns and crime. The 1994 crime bill, for example, provided tighter restrictions on guns and generous funding for enhanced community police strength and prevention programs. The bad news is that some members of Congress have their sights set on killing off these important provisions in favor of funding prison construction and poorly focused block grants.

At this critical juncture, we are over-investing in ineffective quick fixes—three-strikes laws, the death penalty, and boot camps—rather than investing in our burgeoning youth population. Congress and the White House must resist the political temptations of championing the 3 Rs—retribution, retaliation, and revenge. Though it may tend to promote a fourth R—reelection—this bankrupt approach will not be the solution to our impending crime wave.

Even more distressing than the proposed changes in last year's landmark crime control legislation, some critics have, in light of recent crime statistics, suggested that the epidemic of violence may have been overstated through alarmist media hype.

The war against crime is far from won. Complacency and myopia in preparing for the coming crisis of youth crime will almost certainly guarantee a future blood bath—one that will someday make 1995 look like the good old days.

An Effective Response to Teenage Crime Is Possible

Jack Levin published this essay in the Chronicle of Higher Education
*(May 7, 1999) explaining why certain cities have become a model for effective
crime control, while others continue to experience rampant disorder.*

Obscured by the tragic shootings in Littleton, Colorado., and by similar incidents at schools in Paducah, Ky., Pearl, Miss., Jonesboro, Ark., and Springfield, Ore., there is actually encouraging news to report on the subject of crime, especially crime by and among young people in urban areas.

To cite a positive trend, even as we try to fathom the horrific rampage at Littleton's Columbine High School, is not to minimize that calamity. Recognizing effective methods of reducing violence in urban areas may, in fact, even help suburban and rural communities devise pre-emptive programs of their own.

For several years now, the rate of serious crime in localities around the United States has been declining. Indeed, the homicide rate for the nation as a whole recently plummeted to a level that hasn't been seen since the late 1960s. According to the Federal Bureau of Investigation, the rate of murders, for example, fell from 9.4 per 100,000 in 1993 to 6.8 per 100,000 in 1997. Part of the reason for the drop is that as baby boomers mature, they are becoming less likely to engage in criminal—or other risky—behavior.

What's exciting, however, is that the reduction in serious offenses over the past few years includes teenage perpetrators as well. The rate of homicides committed by young people had risen sharply in the late 1980s, but it started dropping in the early 1990s, although it is still above the low levels reached in the 1950s and 1960s.

To explain decreasing teenage crime, studies have focused on a recent decline in the crack epidemic and its accompanying street wars. Experts have also cited zero-tolerance policing, greater handgun control, and other factors. Evidence suggests that all of those phenomena have indeed helped to reduce serious offenses committed by youngsters.

But more important than all of those elements, I believe, is an incipient cultural revolution: a profound change in how Americans meet the needs of children and teenagers, especially in urban areas.

According to my Northeastern University colleague, criminologist James Alan Fox, the murder rate for perpetrators in the 14–17 age group declined to 16.5 per 100,000 in 1997, after having soared to 30.2 per 100,000 in 1993. Similarly, the homicide rate for young adults aged 18 to 24 rose to 41.3 per 100,000 in 1993, then dropped to 33.2 in 1997. Criminologist Alfred Blumstein, of Carnegie Mellon University has suggested that the competition to sell crack and other drugs, after a decade of unabated warfare among youthful dealers, has finally subsided. Many of the victors are, of course, still on the streets, peddling their wares. But the losers are no longer causing trouble for big-city residents—they are, Blumstein says, dead or incarcerated. At the same time, a beefed-up criminal-justice system has taken many handguns off the streets and away from teenage predators.

That explanation is fine, as far as it goes. But there is more to the story. Young people have reduced their involvement in a broad range of serious offenses, even in neighborhoods where crack has been virtually absent, and in types of illegal activities unrelated to crack.

For example, hate crimes usually committed by young people have declined, too. In 1997, the FBI recorded an unprecedented decrease nationwide in assaults, threats, harassments, and vandalism based on hate or bias. And according to the Anti-Defamation League, since 1994 there has been a decline in anti-Semitic hate crimes, including those on college campuses, following a protracted period of increase through the 1980s and early 1990s.

Consider another example. Northeastern University sociologist Benjamin Steiner and I have studied riots in which young people, in groups of 50 or more, looted, damaged property, and/or injured people. We have discovered that nationwide, the number of such acts in urban high schools and colleges, at concerts, or on city streets fell from 23 in the academic year 1990–91 to only nine in 1996–97. Moreover, most of the recent riots we documented could be regarded not as collective expressions of unbridled emotion, but as instrumental and rational acts of protest precipitated by a specific episode—for example, a perceived act of racism, an apparently unjustified arrest by the police, or budget cutbacks with a major impact on a certain group. In other words, even those few riots were not, for the most part, acts of senseless violence.

Although this fact will provide no solace to those grieving in Littleton, violence in elementary and secondary schools is also in decline. Notwithstanding the several highly publicized cases, the American Association of School Administrators reports that violent deaths in schools nationwide fell last year by some 30 percent from 1997. According to a study conducted by the U.S. Department of Education, the number of shooting deaths at schools around the country decreased to 40 during the academic year 1997–98, compared with 55 in 1992–93. Even in the wake of the tragedy in Colorado, the downward trend continued through 1999. It is worth noting that the recent spate of school shootings by teenagers has, by and large, occurred in rural, suburban, and small-town America areas that the crack-cocaine wars hardly touched.

The depth and breadth of the recent turnaround in teenage crime begs for an explanation that includes but goes beyond crack, zero-tolerance policing, gun control, and other important variables. That fuller explanation is that, in urban centers across the country, residents are re-establishing a sense of community as they begin to recognize that they can make a difference in the lives of local youths. At the grassroots level, parents, teachers, psychologists, religious and business leaders, social workers, college students, and police officials are working together to take the glamour out of destructive behavior and to provide constructive activities for after-school hours. Through myriad new programs, adults are giving inner-city teenagers what they have lacked for more than two decades—supervision, structure, guidance, and hope for the future.

Schools have been at the center of effective community efforts to minimize teen violence, taking on responsibilities that families previously performed. More and more high-school principals have adopted a zero-tolerance policy regarding students who carry firearms to school. According to the Education Department, during the 1996–97 school year—the first in which such statistics were compiled—there were an astonishing 6,093 expulsions for firearm violations in schools around the country. In addition, by means of conflict-resolution programs built into the curriculum, many schools are teaching their students what parents used to teach: to have empathy for victims, to control one's anger, and to manage impulsive behavior. Finally, through athletics and other extracurricular programs, schools are increasingly providing what is lacking after the school day ends—adult supervision, guidance, and control.

Schools are not the only institutions that have stepped forward to play guiding roles in children's lives. Churches run athletics and gun buy-back programs. Municipalities have beefed up funds for community policing, and residents have formed partnerships with police. In Boston, which is seen as a model in dealing with youth crime, 34 teenagers were arrested on murder charges in 1990—but the number dropped to three in 1998. During the same period, the city saw a proliferation of programs geared toward at-risk teenagers: the Thousand Black Men Basketball Mentoring Program, Teen Empowerment, Gang Peace, the Ten Point Coalition of urban ministers, the Boston Private Industry Council, Choice Through Education, Baker House, Summer of Opportunity, Operation Night Light, the Street Workers Program, Youth Violence Strike Force...the list goes on.

Not all localities have accomplished as much. While cities such as Boston and New York have enjoyed great success fighting crime by youths and bringing down the associated murder rates, other cities—New Orleans, Baltimore, and Detroit among them have fared less well. They are poorer and cannot afford to devote sufficient resources to law enforcement and social programs, and tend to regard crime as out of control and beyond grassroots intervention.

New Orleans, for example, has a population close to that of Boston—both have about a half-million people. But New Orleans's median household income is $18,000, little more than half of Boston's $30,000. New Orleans has

1,302 police officers patroling the streets, about half the number that Boston has. And New Orleans does not have nearly the number of youth oriented community programs that Boston has. New Orleans's murder rate—though improved somewhat from that of the early 1990s—was seven times as high as Boston's last year. In Baltimore, where more than 300 people have been murdered in each of the past nine years, widespread poverty prevents companies in the city from generating enough summer jobs to keep most local teenagers busy. In contrast, thanks to a combination of public and private contributions, Boston provides in excess of 10,000 summer jobs for teenagers, more than twice Baltimore's total—even though Baltimore's population is roughly 150,000 more than Boston's.

Similarly, unlike Boston, cities such as Detroit and New Orleans simply cannot afford to support a range of alternative-school programs for teenagers between 2 P.M. and 7 P.M. Moreover, in many cities, when youngsters are expelled for carrying a weapon to school, they are likely to walk the streets unsupervised. Typically, Boston schools refer the students they expel for violence to the Public Schools Counseling and Intervention Center, an alternative school that last year alone worked with almost 6,000 youths.

Neither criminologists nor municipalities have paid appropriate heed to the effectiveness of civic programs. It is, after all, easier to focus on easily quantifiable phenomena—homicide rates, arrests on drug or firearm charges, the number of youths incarcerated, the number of police officers on the street—than it is to try to understand how much of a positive effect an army of involved parents and teachers and clerics and mentors can have. Police who are invariably blamed when crime rates go up are understandably quick to take most of the credit when those rates go down, even if a range of other civic factors contribute substantially to the welcome trend. But law-and-order tunnel vision immensely underplays the value, and the potential, of civic activity.

We can all take credit for civic programs that keep some children safer. But then we must also be concerned when, in locales lacking a sustained commitment to such programs, or enough resources to support them, so many other children are left behind.

Moreover, the mayhem of Littleton and similar locales reflects a sad paradox. Because non-urban communities have considered themselves largely immune from the plague of city violence, they haven't organized the kind of pre-emptive civic programs that some metropolises were scared into starting within the past decade. If Littleton has startled the nation's suburban and small town areas out of their complacency, then cities' hard-won experience might benefit the United States as a whole.

In city, town, and country, a stimulating place to go, a constructive thing to do, and family and friends to do it with, are still our best insurance against youths becoming perpetrators, or victims, of violence.

A Longer View on the Rise and Fall of Crime

Following years of declining crime rates, James Alan Fox contributed this opinion piece to the Boston Globe *(April 4, 2000) in which he warns of the dangers of complacency.*

The latest news from the Boston crime front came as quite a shock: five murders over 72 hours, all apparently unconnected events. Capped by this flurry of gun violence, the city closed out the first quarter of 2000 with 11 homicides, placing very much in doubt the chance of improving upon last year's tally of 31 killings.

The recent shooting deaths left many local officials and crime experts scratching their heads. What does it all mean? Is it just a blip, as Police Commissioner Paul F. Evans speculated? Or are we in for another wave of bloodshed like that of a decade ago, when the annual death toll peaked at 152?

Similar questions are being raised in other cities across the country. In New York, after its 1990s renaissance, when murders plummeted by 70 percent, police brass were forced to explain a 6 percent rise in killings for 1999 over 1998. St. Louis reported a 15 percent increase in homicides for 1999 following years of falling murder rates. Washington, D.C., and Dallas both suffered alarming spikes in their murder counts over the first few months of 2000. What a difference a decade makes.

It is critical that these crime statistics be understood in long-term perspective, however. In Norfolk, Va., for example, the police were called to task by city leaders for a sudden 41 percent surge in murders in 1999 over 1998. Yet 1999 had actually been the second-best figure in more than a decade, exceeded only by the 1998 low of 32 violent deaths.

No, the sky is not falling. In light of inevitable short-term fluctuations, it is important that we not overreact to a sudden rebound in crime rates. We should resist the temptation to point an accusatorial finger or to stop doing what has worked. In the stock market, savvy investors learn to wait out short-term shifts. In the crime arena, we should keep our investments in prevention and not rush to increase punishments.

Without overreacting, it is equally important that we recognize the early signs that the new millennium has brought an end to the great 1990s crime-drop party—a decade-long rally in which crime rates dove to 30-year lows virtually everywhere.

It was inevitable that at some point this low point would have been reached. Now is the time to get back to work—not with the unlikely goal of reducing crime further, but of not allowing it to increase very much.

Regrettably, complacency seems to have settled in across America, replacing the sense of urgency that characterized the early 1990s. Sure, lawfulness and order, rather than lawlessness and disorder, have become the norm. Yet we may have become too comfortable that crime trends were moving in the right direction and have diverted our attention elsewhere.

Crime rates, however, are rather resilient. Without sustained effort, they can and will rebound. And there is reason for concern. Even with the decline since 1993, youth crime levels in the United States remain high. The rate of killing by teens, for example, may be down 50 percent from its 1993 peak, but it is up 50 percent from its 1985 trough. The glass is half empty, not half full. We may have won a battle or two, but the war is far from over.

In addition, we have a new crop of teenagers every few years, each looking to express its desire for excitement and rebellion. The next group entering the high-risk ages will be much larger. While we may have been successful in sending a strong antiviolence message to today's youth, they will not necessarily pass it on.

Looking long-term, there is actually good news ahead. Overshadowing the expanding population of teens and young adults, the fastest-growing segment of the population are the seniors, whose involvement with violent crime ranks lowest across age groups.

Yet when is it ever the case that all else remains equal? We shouldn't bet on lower homicide rates. Instead, we should prepare now for the violent crime storm about which crime prognosticators have warned and keep the crime-drop party hats handy to celebrate when we successfully avert it.

Spousal Murders Are Declining

Notwithstanding appropriate concern for domestic violence, James Alan Fox argues in this column for the Boston Globe *(November 9, 1997) that various social and legal interventions have saved lives.*

In spite of the recent slayings of Elaine Donahue of Reading and Annie Glenn of Lowell, domestic homicide is actually declining in Massachusetts and the United States. Over the past 15 years, the number of American women murdered by their husbands or ex-husbands has dropped by a third, from an estimated 1,500 per year in and around 1980 to about 1,000 last year. During this same time, the incidence of men killed by their wives and ex-wives—often a protective response to years of physical or sexual abuse— has plummeted by two-thirds, from about 1,200 per year in the early 1980s to less than 400 in 1996.

The causes of the precipitous drop around the country have little to do with stiff sentencing or tough punishment. Rather, the decline largely reflects the increased range of social and legal services—from shelters for battered women to temporary restraining orders—available to help women escape an abusive relationship before becoming a murder statistic.

In addition, as a society we have become far more enlightened about domestic abuse. We no longer blame the victim of domestic violence, which encouraged her to internalize feelings of failure and guilt for an unhappy and unsuccessful marriage.

The trigger event in domestic slayings typically involves some form of argument. More than two-thirds of the fatal attacks between intimates stem from a dispute over money, jealousy, or involve some form of intoxication.

For this reason, initiatives designed to keep loaded guns out of the hands of angry or abusive partners are worthy and wise, and are paying off. Over the past 15 years, the drop in spousal homicides involving guns has been especially pronounced, down by more than half. We should continue to reinforce our attempts to convince American men and women that guns in the home often do more harm than good.

Finally, changes in law enforcement policies and practices have also had an impact on levels of spousal homicide. Increasingly, police respond to domestic quarrels by removing or even arresting an instigator of violence. These interventions have served to reduce the number of times that domestic violence has escalated into homicide.

A critic might note that the downturn in domestic homicide to some degree reflects changing family relationships in America. Increasingly divorce and separation have become alternatives to murder. Moreover, although instances of boyfriend-girlfriend murder do occur, marital ties and dependencies are far stronger—sometimes in a negative way. Even so, the decline in spousal murder is so significant that it is much more than a statistical artifact. We can legitimately credit the progress made by domestic violence advocacy groups.

We all should feel outraged when someone is murdered by a spouse. We should insist on appropriate sanctions to express our anger and intolerance. However, any thought that tough penalties can lower future trends in domestic killing fails to recognize how prevention succeeds while punishment fails to deter.

PART II

YOUTH HOMICIDE

Translating Concern About Juvenile Violence into Collective Action

In this piece written for the Philadelphia Inquirer *(February 29, 1996), Jack Levin suggests that America is on the verge of a major cultural shift in the manner in which it treats youth.*

Whether we realize it or not, our society is at the threshold of a major cultural revolution. At the grassroots level and up, the popular sentiment against violent crime is on the rise.

Americans everywhere are addressing the issue like never before, holding conferences, lectures and workshops, phoning radio talk shows, discussing the problem with friends and relatives, and writing their representatives in Washington.

Parallels can be found in our nation's changing attitudes toward cigarette smoking. Prior to the Surgeon General's 1968 report linking tobacco with cancer, smoking was widely regarded as fashionable and stylish. But more than 30 years later, the campaign has discredited smoking and has stigmatized smokers.

However, although the anti-smoking campaign reduced the consumption of cigarettes among adults, it essentially failed to convert young people. Every year, an additional 4,000 teenagers take up the smoking habit.

In the same way, teenagers aren't likely to be touched by a cultural revolution just because it asks that they become less destructive. Most feel immune from long-term consequences—whether contracting lung cancer or going to prison.

While the homicide rate among their parents has dropped since 1985, the rate of murder committed by teenagers has more than doubled.

According to criminologist James Alan Fox, younger and younger teens are becoming increasingly involved in serious violent crimes—carjackings, spraying bullets into crowds, and killing for the sake of a leather jacket or a pair of sneakers.

Unlike anti-smoking campaigns, however, the success of a cultural revolution concerning violence depends not on teenagers, but on their parents, their teachers, their clergy, their employers, and their neighbors.

In combating, violent behavior, our youngsters will change only to the extent that the adults in their lives change first.

Years ago, researchers conducted a famous study that examined the effect of illumination on the productivity of a group of factory workers at Western Electric. First, researchers turned up the lights and worker productivity increased.

Then, researchers turned down the lights to approximate pale moonlight, but productivity increased even more. Their conclusion was surprising: degree of illumination had nothing to do with productivity; it was actually a result of the increased attention these workers were given by the researchers.

Participating in an "important" experiment had made the workers feel special. Researchers called their unexpected finding the Hawthorne Effect, because of the area in which it was located.

We need a Hawthorne Effect on juvenile violence that translates widespread concern into collective action. In response to severe cutbacks by state and federal government, this means working even harder to repair the moral, social, and economic damage done to our youngsters and to take the glamour out of their destructive behavior.

To a limited extent, cultural change has already left its mark. Local institutions have sponsored some impressive programs aimed at local youngsters—for example, gun buy-back programs, conflict resolution and mentoring programs in the schools, college scholarships, summer jobs programs, and after-school activities sponsored by local companies.

In order to avert disaster, however, much more of the same will be needed. Teenagers who have been routinely ignored, unsupervised, and left to fend for themselves must discover that adults are ready to help.

They must be given healthy alternatives to violence that cause them to feel important and special—because somebody besides a drug dealer cares about them.

Hurting Animals Is an Important Clue

Arnold Arluke and Jack Levin published a version of this essay in the
Boston Herald *(September 1, 1997) in which they urge that animal
abuse be taken more seriously—and not just for the sake of the family pet.*

A Massachusetts woman recently came home to find that her 14-year-old son had crushed her small dog's testicles and caused it severe spinal injuries. In rural Iowa, three teenaged boys broke into an animal shelter, where they bludgeoned to death 16 cats. And a Florida resident clubbed to death a neighbor's 11-year-old Rottweiler.

Every year, thousands of animals around the country are reported victims of malicious cruelty. If these crimes were committed against children, the abusers would likely face stiff penalties in court, but not so in the case of animal offenses.

Indeed, animal abusers appear to be getting away with murder, figuratively speaking. For example, according to a three-year study of animal cruelty in Massachusetts we recently wrote with Carter Luke of the Massachusetts Society for the Prevention of Cruelty to Animals (MSPCA), even in the most extreme cases of animal cruelty a majority of the abusers are not found guilty. Most don't even get to trial. When they do, they typically get a slap on the wrist.

Only one in 10 of those convicted receive jail sentences. And fines are minimal when imposed, averaging $132.

The presumed indifference of criminal justice professionals to animal abuse in part reflects the fact that society values animals less than people. In addition, there are serious human issues to address in the criminal justice system, such as homicide and rape, that eclipse other concerns.

Most important, incidents of animal cruelty are typically viewed as isolated crimes having no relationship to other human behavior, such as violence against people. The attitude among criminal justice personnel too frequently seems to be: "Suppose we make a concerted effort to wipe out animal cruelty—so what? When the money is spent, we will still be left fighting rape, murder, assault, burglary, and drug abuse."

But research strongly suggests that understanding the causes and consequences of violence toward animals may be important in the effort to fight crime against humans. A link has long been suspected between cruelty to animals and human violence. In the 1960s, for example, psychiatrist John Macdonald first suggested that those individuals who later become homicidal begin in childhood by torturing small animals. Subsequent research on violent prisoners and abusive domestic partners supported Macdonald's position.

Our MSPCA study is the first of its kind to look at the relationship between violence against animals and crime in the general population. We had unprecedented access to MSPCA law enforcement files, tracking the criminal records of convicted animal abusers over 20 years and comparing them to "next-door neighbors" with no known history of animal abuse.

The findings were dramatic. People who abused animals were five times more likely than those who did not to commit violent crimes against people—to assault, rape, or rob them.

Surprisingly, animal abuse was found to be linked with many types of nonviolent crimes as well. Abusers were four times more likely than non-abusers to commit property crimes and three times more likely to be arrested for drug-related offenses and disorderly conduct.

What can be done to reduce animal abuse? In the face of such evidence linking it with other crimes, we urge professionals—district attorneys, judges, police officers, doctors, social workers, teachers, and ministers—to take appropriate measures. According to a recent national survey, 71 percent of adults favor making animal abuse a felony. Eighty-one percent approve strengthening the enforcement of cruelty laws. About 83 percent favor teachers, social workers, animal welfare officers, and law enforcement officials sharing information on juveniles who abuse animals as an early warning of criminal behavior. And 75 percent support the establishment of a system for tracking adult animal cruelty offenders as a tool for identifying other kinds of likely violent offenses.

This study also carries a strong message for parents. Not every child who tortures animals grows up to become a killer. Yet, animal abuse is clearly a warning sign that deserves to be taken seriously in order to intervene before it is too late.

Our MSPCA study provides strong evidence to support this view. The lesson is clear enough: By taking animal cruelty more seriously, we might help ourselves.

Our New Pastime

We wrote this piece in anticipation of Major League Baseball's All-Star Game, arguing that the baseball industry has struck out in dealing with youngsters. The essay appeared in the Pittsburgh Post-Gazette *(July 12, 1994), the day of the game.*

Major league baseball used to be "America's pastime" for kids of all ages. But in the interest of TV ratings (not to mention beer sales), it has become "America's primetime"—most games are now played under the lights. Even this month's All-Star Classic at Three Rivers Stadium is pastime alright— past the time when many young fans can stay up to watch it. And children permitted to catch this year's July showcase will probably not be so lucky on school nights in October when the World Series is telecast well after dark.

A generation ago, at a time when children still counted, many young fans would go down to Forbes Field to sit in the bleachers and hope to get autographs from the star players. (Autographs were, of course, free back then.) Other kids would spend their afternoons rooting for the Pirates on radio or television. Inspired by the skillful performance of Roberto Clemente or Willie Stargell, they would then head out to the sandlot and imitate their heroes on the field.

As baseball has become less accessible to them, today's children have filled the entertainment void with violence. On television, hardball has been replaced by *Hardcopy, Inside Baseball* by *Inside Edition.* Rather than sneak transistor radios into class to listen to the big game, many kids today are sneaking in guns and knives. To them, "hit and run" is associated more with a quick get away from a crime scene than with a baseball tactic for avoiding a double play.

In the meantime, social scientists and children's advocates are criticizing the role of television in contributing to spiraling rates of youth crime. Prompted by a Congressional investigation, top executives at the four networks conceded to provide viewer warnings for programs with content so violent that parents would be advised to consider whether the program is too mature for their youngsters.

Reactions to this industry initiative have been appropriately critical. The plan assumes that parents will be home to see the warning flash upon the screen and change the channel. But in an era of single-parent families and dual-career households, this is *Fantasy Island*. If more parents were actually available to monitor their children's viewing habits, television would not be the problem that it is.

Notwithstanding the debate over whether Congress let the television industry off too easy, the viewer warning solution misses the point entirely. Even if parents heed the warnings and supervise their children's viewing choices, what healthy and entertaining alternatives do they have? Beavis and Butthead? Mortal Kombat? The trials and tribulations of O. J. Simpson?

In order to get children to tune out violence, we must give them something better to tune into. TV might consider taking its cue from the movies.

It is true that youngsters will flock to violent films like *Lethal Weapon* and *Terminator;* it is also true that they will often shun "kids' movies" that are not rated at least PG-13. But the popularity of recent films like *Rookie of the Year, Little Big League,* and *Angels in the Outfield* indicates that kids are drawn to sports films, no matter what the rating.

So, it's not that kids have abandoned baseball—it's that baseball has abandoned the kids. We are not naive enough to suggest that we can bring back all the day games, the free autographs, or even the half-price tickets for children. But we certainly can have a major league "Game of the Day," televised nationally, everyday of the week.

Of course, the issue is much larger than just putting afternoon baseball back on the tube. For the sake of short-term economic savings, we have closed down the neighborhood movie houses, community recreation centers, and local swimming pools. To control taxes, we have neglected the zoos, playgrounds, ballfields and lakes.

Fortunately, some community leaders have begun to recognize the value of sports as an alternative to violence. In many cities across the country, for example, midnight basketball leagues have been established to encourage gang members to put down their guns and pick up a basketball. This is a good idea, but it sends the wrong message. Why does a teenager first have to be a gang member in order to make the team? Shouldn't we have daytime basketball leagues and summer baseball programs, with top-of-the-line equipment and dedicated coaches, for kids of all ages, even if they haven't yet been drawn to violence?

So violence on television may be a problem, but it is hardly *the* problem. When it comes to reducing teenage violence, boredom and idleness are at the core. We can't just change the channel; we have to change our priorities.

Who's Minding the Kids?

In this essay, which appeared in the Boston Globe *(December 20, 1993), Jack Levin makes the case that the problem of juvenile violence goes well beyond the few youngsters who actually commit murder.*

The headlines scream daily of hideous crimes—driveby shootings, carjackings, and senseless murders—committed by our nation's teenagers. What makes violence so appealing to so many youngsters? Why is it that, in many quarters around the country, guns have replaced leather jackets and CD players as status symbols of choice?

According to the FBI, the number of homicides committed by youngsters in their early teens has skyrocketed lately. Between 1985 and 1991, arrest rates for homicide increased among 13- and 14-year-old males by 140 percent; among 15-year-old males by 217 percent.

Actually, the problem is even worse than these dreadful statistics might suggest. While relatively few of our youngsters are committing hideous murders, they are being tolerated—perhaps even honored—by their friends and classmates. Millions of teenagers may not be able to shoot or stab someone themselves, but they are fully capable of looking on as others do.

Attorney Marsha Kazarosian recently filed a suit against the Winnecunnet, N.H., school district on behalf of the families of the three youngsters convicted in the murder of Greg Smart in Derry, N.H. Kazarosian claims that Pam Smart's love affair with her 15-year-old student was made possible because she was unsupervised by the Winnecunnet High School administration—that somebody in charge should have been keeping a watchful eye on her.

Whether or not school officials should have known, it appears that they may have been the only ones at Winnecunnet High who didn't.

Statements during the course of the police investigation indicate that at least one month before the Derry police finally broke the case, the corridors of Winnecunnet High were abuzz with rumors implicating the three students and their teacher. Yet nobody bothered to inform an adult.

More incredibly, later statements to law enforcement officials indicate that students at Winnecunnet High were talking about Greg Smart's murder for two months before it actually occurred. With a simple phone call, any one of them might have prevented a murder. But nobody wanted to snitch on a classmate.

Too many of our teenagers have become desensitized to the consequences of violence. They have been raised on a steady diet of slasher films filled with gory scenes of sex, murder, and mayhem. After school they come home to an empty house, where they spend hours daily listening to rap and heavy-metal lyrics or watching MTV videos in which violence is glorified. For economic reasons, more and more of our teenagers are left unsupervised after school and during vacations.

The murder might have happened in Derry, N.H., but it could have been anywhere. Marsha Kazarosian's lawsuit reflects an unpleasant truth about American society today. It isn't that TV movies and popular music are so powerful. It is that our traditional institutions have become so weak. Our schools, religions, and families have lost their moral authority. We have allowed the peer group to fill their place in our youngsters' lives.

Mr. and Mrs. Bueller's Night in Jail

We wrote this column for the Christian Science Monitor *(December 28, 1999) in reaction to a growing movement in America toward holding parents legally responsible for their children's misbehavior.*

In the 1986 film classic *Ferris Bueller's Day Off,* actor Matthew Broderick asked casually, "How can I possibly be expected to handle school on a day like this?" Playing hooky, formerly regarded as little more than an adolescent prank, is nowadays prompting a decidedly punitive response.

Today's lawmakers would be looking to haul Ferris's parents off to jail for failing to ensure his attendance at school. According to recent data, school absenteeism has become an epidemic. For many of our children, skipping school is the largest part of their daily routine. Gone are the days of reading, writing, and 'rithmetic, now replaced by an extended version of recess.

In Detroit, for example, 63,000 students—more than one-third of the city's public school population—cut at least 30 days of classes last year. In New York City, 65,000 students were chronically absent without a legitimate excuse. "Where are these kids' parents?" we collectively ask.

It has long been fashionable to point fingers at parents when their kids misbehave. Ever since Sigmund Freud, we've been quick to scapegoat parents for their children's aberrant or delinquent behavior.

Bad kids have been seen inevitably as the products of bad homes and bad parenting. Thus, communities across the country are going so far as to enact and enforce parental responsibility laws for a range of adolescent acting out, from burglary to gun crimes. Now we can add truancy to the list. Many states are counting on legal sanctions to coerce and scare parents into taking more responsibility for their truant youngsters.

In February, when their children failed to show up for class, six mothers from Springfield, Ill. were threatened with 30 days in jail. Last May, a grand jury in Brewton, Ala., indicted the 10 parents of truant teenagers on charges punishable by three months behind bars. And the parents of 67 out-of-school children in Detroit face prospects of being incarcerated for up to 90 days.

Other states are now in the process of passing bills that would toughen the penalties against parents. In Ohio, such legislation has gone through the Senate and awaits review by the House. In Virginia, a get-tough-on-parents law was recently signed by the governor.

Holding parents legally responsible for their children's chronic absenteeism sounds better than it is. First, such laws send the wrong message to wayward youngsters who are all too eager to escape the blame for their misconduct. By aiming the legal sanctions at mom and dad, we teach children that they need not feel personally responsible for their truancy—that only their parents need to change, not them.

Even worse, parental responsibility laws may backfire by persuading more parents to distance themselves from their difficult youngsters rather than face the possibility—if they fail—of being fined or spending time behind bars. Why take the risk yourself when you can let the state take over if you're having problems with your child? This may mean less diligent parenting, not more.

At the very time in our history when the family is fast becoming an endangered species, let's consider a wholly different approach to wayward parents. We should assist them, not assail them. Rather than making mom and dad the truant officers of society, we should take a more positive approach to the problem of truancy.

We ought to be generating programs and policies that support parents to deal with their incorrigible youngsters. We might also try making school more appealing by bringing back art, drama, music, and athletics. Frequently referred to disparagingly as the "frills," these are the very activities that used to make school interesting enough to attend—even without being forced by parents or the law.

PART **III**

SCHOOL SHOOTINGS

Again!: School Attacks Show Need for New Strategies

In this article for the Boston Globe *(May 24, 1998), James Alan Fox analyzes recent school shootings—their causes and possible solutions.*

Last week, it happened twice. On Tuesday, a Fayetteville, Tenn., high school senior shot and killed a classmate over a romantic rivalry. And on Thursday, a Springfield, Ore., freshman armed with a .22-caliber semiautomatic rifle turned his high school cafeteria into a battle zone. The boy, 15, had been suspended a day earlier for having a gun in his locker.

There is irony in the recent contagion of schoolyard homicide, which has left 14 students and two teachers dead since December. Serious violence among teenagers has actually dropped nationally since 1993. Many American cities have registered significant declines in their murder rates, including juvenile killings.

But even as rates of urban youth violence are declining, suburban and rural areas are seeing signs of increasing gang affiliation and identification. And many of the recent attacks have been in relatively small communities.

The lesson from them, including a March assault in Jonesboro, Ark., by two boys, ages 11 and 13, is that the country still has a long way to go before it can claim victory over youth violence. The alleged assailants in Jonesboro hid in the woods to ambush their middle school classmates.

A closer examination of crime trends reveals that recent declines are predominantly among minority youth in large urban centers—cities such as Boston, New York, and Chicago that have directed intensive enforcement efforts against street gangs and illegal guns.

And though the rate of killings by teenagers is down from several years ago, the rate in 1996 was still twice as high as in 1985, before the spread of crack cocaine and guns, particularly in big cities, led to rampant disorder.

The acute conditions associated with the fiercely competitive crack market of the late 1980s proved to be short-term. Yet the more long-term and chronic problems associated with poorly supervised and alienated youth who have access to deadly weapons and violent entertainment continue. Shootings such as those in Jonesboro and Springfield, where two students were killed and 17 were injured, are extreme, but they are the tip of an iceberg of antisocial behavior increasingly exhibited by children.

The latest episode of schoolyard violence has heightened concern over youngsters with firearms. In fact, the entire growth in teenage murder has been with guns, rather than knives, clubs or fists. It has long been true that teenagers are often impulsive, impatient, and imprudent, but now they are better armed. A greater emphasis on firearm restrictions for juveniles, including gun tracing, confiscation, and firearms safety, could help to reduce youth access to deadly weapons.

Part of the seemingly casual attitude toward violence exhibited by youngsters can be linked to a popular culture saturated with violent messages in which revenge is a dominant theme. While the issue of television and film violence has been widely discussed, these passive forms of entertainment are tame compared with the more active participation provided by video and computer games.

Rather than just sit on the living room couch and witness a bloodbath on the TV screen, a child can cybernetically kill on demand—and perhaps learn to enjoy it—through the games on the market. The violence is make-believe, of course, but with multimedia and advanced graphics, the line between virtual reality and stark reality can become thin.

The fundamental problem, however, is not so much what our children are watching, but who is watching our children. Guns, gangs, and glorified violence have filled part of the void left by the withdrawal of adults from the lives and activities of children. Negative social and cultural forces have become more threatening precisely because the positive socializing forces of family, school, religion, and neighborhood have weakened.

This is not to place full blame on parents for the increased problem of unruly and unsupervised youth. While some parents are ill-prepared or unmotivated for the important task of raising children, most parents are well-meaning and would like to have a greater role in their children's lives. Many families lack the support network to control and guide their children. In some neighborhoods, peer and gang influences can overpower the best efforts of dedicated parents. Parents need help.

Children spend too little time engaged in structured activities with positive role models, and too much time hanging out or watching a few savage killings on television. Bored and idle, they have too much time on their hands, too much time to kill. This concern is clearly reflected in the time-of-day patterns of juvenile violence. The prime time for juvenile crime begins after the dismissal bell rings, from 2 P.M. to 8 P.M., when nearly half of such crime occurs. Expanding after-school programs, lengthening or restructuring the school day, and other strategies to engage children positively would reduce the problem of excessive idle time.

It is not coincidental that the recent shootings occurred at schools. Notwithstanding research suggesting that most schools do not experience serious violence, schooltime itself can present risks. Not only do children congregate in large numbers while at school, thereby creating opportunities for conflict, but the setting can sometimes breed feelings of inadequacy, anxiety, fear, hostility, rejection, and boredom.

For some vengeful or alienated children, school can represent an ideal place, logistically and symbolically, for getting even or settling a score. School personnel, in turn, are in an ideal position to observe and respond to troubled children in ways far more creative than suspension.

The recent spate of school shootings also has rekindled public debate over juvenile justice. Many people are particularly outraged over the prospect that the alleged shooters in Jonesboro could be released from custody as early as their 18th birthdays.

There is universal agreement that juvenile offenders must be punished. At the same time, society must fully consider the special nature of youthful offending—even murder. Teenagers may look like adults, dress like adults, act like adults, even shoot like adults, but they reason like children. Making the juvenile justice system more just is one thing, but diminishing it is quite another. Expanding juvenile penalties will go a long way to assuage public concern without entirely sacrificing young lives that could be salvaged.

It is critical that legislative responses to juvenile crime maintain a balance between punishment and prevention. Without sufficient attention to prevention, future demographics—specifically, the projected increase in the teenage population—could make matters worse. But the nation needs to act now—by reinvesting in schools, recreation, and other programs for youth. It is far easier and considerably less expensive to build the child than to rebuild the teenager.

Even with our desire to "do something" through programs or legislation in response to recent schoolyard tragedies, some perspective is sorely needed on the level of risk of schoolyard violence. Many more children are killed or maimed each year in automobile and bicycle accidents while traveling between home and school than are shot by an armed classmate. Parents concerned about their youngster's safety are better advised to focus on seat belts and bicycle helmets than on metal detectors at school doors.

At the same time, society can learn much about more ordinary forms of juvenile violence by focusing on extraordinary cases in Springfield, Jonesboro, West Paducah, Ky., and Pearl, Miss. We should use these rare though devastating episodes to inform and motivate public and private responses to the needs of children. By doing so, we might not necessarily prevent another Springfield but we would surely improve the lives and well-being of children.

Schools Learning a Grim Lesson

Writing days after the Columbine High School tragedy for the Boston Globe *(April 25, 1999), we focus on those aspects of school that make it the safest place in the lives of most children.*

By contrast to last year's string of school shootings, this academic year had been quiet enough to move the issue of school violence to the back burner. However, any sense of security vanished last Tuesday when two masked gunmen, dressed in black trench coats and reportedly members of a small fraternity of outcasts, pummeled a suburban Denver high school with gunfire and explosives. By the time the smoke and panic had cleared, 14 students and one teacher were dead, and many more injured.

In the wake of this latest and largest episode of school violence, many Americans—parents and politicians alike—are calling for steps to make schools more secure. Even before this most recent incident, President Clinton announced a $65 million initiative to assist schools in hiring 2,000 officers to serve as security patrols.

More and more schools are beginning to resemble armed camps. Police and security guards patrol the hallways, looking with suspicion for students who might hate their teachers and classmates enough to seek revenge with a loaded gun. In many high schools, metal detectors are strategically located at entrances, so that students carrying weapons can be disarmed. A Georgia legislator went as far as to propose arming teachers and training them to shoot in order to deter potentially violent students.

While motivated by genuine concern for the safety of our youngsters, the focus on reducing school violence may be misplaced. For one thing, many observers tend to separate the school from its community context and treat it as an island. Yet neighborhoods in which handguns are readily available to young people also tend to experience gun violence in their classrooms. Communities which contain extreme poverty, high levels of transiency, unemployment, and crime also tend to suffer high levels of school violence.

Notwithstanding last week's catastrophe in Colorado, the widespread concern for school safety is largely a reflection of the distorted images presented by the mass media. We see in the news not the representative cases, but the extraordinary ones—mass murders, eleven-year-old children who seek to get even with classmates, and schoolyard snipers. If a juvenile killing happens on the streets, it is unlikely to be reported nationally. However, if the same murder occurs in the classroom, it will make the headlines in newspapers across the country.

It is tragic that nearly four dozen children were killed last year at or outside their schools. But given the 50 million schoolchildren in America, the chances are literally one in a million that any given student will become a victim of schoolyard murder. In fact, more children are killed each year in bicycle or car accidents while traveling between home and school than are murdered by an armed classmate.

For most of our children, the school hours are actually the safest part of the day. A recent national study indicated that about 90 percent of public schools experience no serious violent crimes during the school year; 84 percent of all high school students are not involved in any physical confrontations with schoolmates, and only 3 percent of all teachers report that they have been physically attacked by a student. Another study found that half of violent crimes committed by teenagers occur between the after-school hours of 2 P.M. and 8 P.M., yet only 16 percent happen between 9 A.M. and 2 P.M.— when our kids are in their classrooms, not on the streets or in their homes.

We have been so obsessed with short-term issues of school security that we have failed to notice the effective long-term measures that educators have taken in order to reduce violence and conflict. Many school districts now maintain zero-tolerance policies regarding weapons, summarily expelling or suspending a student who brings a gun to school for whatever reason, offensive or defensive. Not only have they removed gun-toting teens from the classrooms, but many jurisdictions have initiated alternative programs for such youngsters, in which they are given the assistance and support they so desperately need.

Many schools are also teaching violence prevention and conflict resolution skills to their students. Twenty-five years ago, parents would have assumed the responsibility for teaching anger management, impulse control, and even empathy; now, the schools are more likely to do so.

The efforts of the schools have paid off big time, not only in combating violence at school, but also in generalizing such strategies to other areas of life. Lessons learned in the classroom are successfully being applied to resolving disagreements on the playgrounds after school and even to reducing arguments between siblings at home.

Most important, many schools are providing their students with supervision and structure. Schools—even the worst schools—provide a degree of adult supervision, guidance, and structure which may be missing in other areas of a child's everyday life. There are the schools with small classes and personalized attention, with counselors, psychologists, and social workers on staff, with parents, grandparents, and college student volunteers who

come in during the school day to offer tutoring, mentoring, and peer medi-
ation. These are the schools in which students are offered a wide range of
activities to keep them busy, thinking, and alive. And these are the schools
which provide clear and fairly enforced rules governing student conduct.

As the Colorado school tragedy reminds us in the most alarming way,
school violence is a serious issue which deserves to be addressed in a serious
manner. The murder of even one child is, of course, unacceptable. But, by
exaggerating the problem and making it the focal point of public policy
based on a few extraordinary cases, we lose an opportunity to craft effective
responses to the problem of teen violence on our streets, in our neighborhoods, and at home. We also fail to recognize the large number of schools in
which violence is simply not a major issue.

So, what can be done to assure that our streets are safe from youth violence? Do what the schools do—get rid of the guns, socialize our youngsters
to have self-control and empathy, and provide them with the supervision and
guidance they deserve to have. In short, give our youngsters healthy alternatives to violence.

School Violence: Easy Solutions That Won't Work and Difficult Ones That Will

In the wake of Columbine and other school shootings, a number of anti-violence measures were implemented in schools across America. In this piece, a version of which was published in the Boston Sunday Globe *(August 22, 1999), we critically evaluate these strategies.*

As the school year begins, the horror of last spring's devastation at Columbine High in Littleton, Colorado is still fresh in our minds and heavy on our hearts. This tragedy as well as other school shootings in communities from Jonesboro, Arkansas to Edinboro, Pennsylvania, have caused parents everywhere to be deeply concerned about their children's safety, and understandably so.

In fact, a recent national survey conducted by Fight Crime, Invest in Kids confirms what many of us have suspected—for parents, it's "safety first." Over half of the respondents who volunteered concerns about the back-to-school season cited school safety as their leading worry, well ahead of issues related to academic quality and the availability of educational resources.

Is there anything that can be done to address parents' fears? Plenty can and should be done to stem the tide of school violence. Unfortunately, those policies and practices that seem to be the most attractive to parents and politicians alike are the easy and quick fixes—bad ideas that simply won't work or may even cause more problems than they solve. By contrast, there are several effective and lasting strategies—typically, difficult solutions that may take time, effort, and money to implement, but are the most promising in order to reduce the scourge of schoolyard bloodshed.

EASY BUT BAD IDEAS FOR REDUCING SCHOOL VIOLENCE

Run public service announcements: President Clinton recently launched a series of TV ads depicting scared youngsters pleading with their schoolmates to behave, which are designed to encourage kids to talk to their parents about violence. Not only do they add to the massive stockpile of frightening media publicity already given to school violence, but these spots might actually inspire rejected and alienated teenagers to terrorize other students in order to get revenge. They, too, would just love to make their classmates beg, plead, and cry.

Install metal detectors: Metal detectors are hardly foolproof; there are many other ways in which a student can smuggle weapons past these devices. Besides, a vengeful student can still kill his victims in the school yard (like in Jonesboro, Arkansas) or even on the bus. Even worse, the presence of metal detectors may lull concerned teachers and parents into believing falsely that guns are no longer a problem at school.

Say "no" to knapsacks: Some schools are banning all but mesh book-bags so that concealed weapons become visible. And one school district in Florida has decided to provide all students with two sets of books, one for school and one for home. What's next—strip searches?

Place more cops in the halls: President Clinton wants to spend millions on providing the schools with armed security patrols. Besides the fact that Columbine High School had one, this would make schools seem more like armed camps and would increase levels of fear and anxiety to the point where learning becomes impossible.

"Katie bar the door": A number of schools have decided to lock all school entrances and exits in order to limit access. A new school construction project near us has been modified to eliminate doors altogether. We shudder to think what might happen if a fire should occur or even if students should attempt to flee from a student who does start shooting.

Arm the faculty: The National Rifle Association as well as a number of political and civic leaders are proposing concealed weapons for teachers and administrators. This will surely backfire. Rather than acting as a deterrent, it could encourage an angry student to shoot it out with the faculty. The same policy might even prompt an irate and frustrated teacher to use a gun, rather than a verbal reprimand, on a belligerent student. Let's not confuse the NEA with the NRA; marksmanship in schools is about A's and B's, not guns and ammo. More generally, teachers should be educating students, not executing them.

Observe telltale warning signs and respond aggressively: There are plenty of warning signs that are, however, only clear after the fact. Using one of several publicized lists of red flags would identify hundreds of thousands of would-be shooters, well over 99 percent of whom wouldn't harm anyone. In fact, targeting these "misfits" or "social outcasts" could backfire by further singling them out in a negative way. They would feel, "Not only are the students against me, but so are the teachers and the principal."

Maintain zero-tolerance for threats and weapons: Schools across America have instituted zero-tolerance policies for threats and weapons.

Applied rigidly, this has resulted in the suspension of elementary school children in Georgia for making a list of people they wanted to hurt (including the Spice Girls and Barney, the purple dinosaur); a girl in Utah who brought the wrong lunch bag to school which contained an apple and a paring knife; and a second grader in Maryland who made a gun out of construction paper. Zero-ignorance and a rational level of tolerance make far greater sense in practice.

Require school uniforms: Although there may be a short-term effect in the long-run school uniforms simply don't work. If kids have the desire to identify their tastes and cliques through apparel, they can always resort to hair styles, tattoos, or other means of distinguishing themselves. Of course, banning black trench coats, as has been proposed, would only force certain kids to choose another form of expression and identification.

DIFFICULT BUT EFFECTIVE STRATEGIES FOR REDUCING SCHOOL VIOLENCE

Increase after school programs or lengthen the school day. With structure and regular supervision, the rate of violence in schools (literally one homicide per one million schoolchildren) is lower than anywhere else—the playground, the neighborhood, the mall, even the home. The prime time for teenage crime consists of the hours between 2 P.M. and 7 P.M.—after school is out and before working parents get home. The supervision provided by an expanded school day would greatly curtail juvenile violence.

Bring back the "frills" in school (violins rather then violence): in the wake of various taxpayer revolts, many of the extracurricular options (band, chorus, drama, various sports, computer clubs, etc.) were eliminated in a return to the basics. This has made school increasingly distasteful and unpleasant for those kids who fail to excel in academics, but could feel good about their achievements in other areas. Ideally, these activities should be integrated better throughout an expanded school day.

Decrease school size (as well as class size): Schools like Columbine High, with well over a thousand students, fail to capture any sense of community. Short of a basketball championship to rally the students, only a tragic shooting seems to bring everyone together. Schools limited to about 500 students are far better in fostering a collective environment, though they may cost a bit more.

Increase school staffing and reduce student/staff ratio: If school teachers and guidance counselors are ever going to be effective in identifying and responding to troubled youth, they need a much smaller "caseload." Also, increasing the pay scale for school staff will enhance the attractiveness of this role for the most talented individuals. While we're at it, we might re-examine ways in which tenure should be modified to eliminate disaffected teachers. Given adequate resources, good teachers and counselors are able to identify students who are being unmercifully harassed and intervene before it is too late.

Teach conflict resolution skills early on: While many schools have introduced conflict resolution programs at the high school level or even in middle school years, the most effective programs start in elementary school when styles and patterns of peer-interaction are still developing. Recent evidence shows that students who graduate from elementary school programs with these methods integrated in the curriculum are far more successful in middle school. Moreover, the lessons a child learns from conflict resolution programs are often generalized to arguments on the playground after school and to disagreements with siblings at home.

Provide alternative programs for students who are suspended for carrying weapons: Even with the modest decline last year, still thousands of students are suspended or expelled every year for carrying guns and other weapons to school. Unfortunately, less than half of the states have alternative programs for such students—clearly the most troublesome and troubled segment of the student population. This means that many dangerous youngsters, prevented from sitting in a classroom, are instead roaming the streets without supervision.

Even with our desire to "do something" programmatically or legislatively in response to recent schoolyard tragedies, some perspective on the level of risk is sorely needed. In a relative sense, more children are killed or maimed each year in automobile and bicycle accidents while traveling between home and school than are murdered or shot by an armed classmate. Parents concerned about their youngsters' safety would be most advised, therefore, to focus on seat belts and bicycle helmets than bullet-proof school uniforms or metal detectors at the school door.

Rampant concern about school safety does, however, provide an opportunity—an opportunity to invest in kids. We may or may not be able to prevent the next Jonesboro or Littleton, but in the process of trying we certainly can enhance the quality of life for all of our young people. The choice is ours: Pay for our children now or pray for the victims later.

A Few Bad Apples

We published a version of this argument against the use of prediction devices for identifying would-be school shooters in the Boston Sunday Herald *(September 19, 1999).*

In the aftermath of the Columbine tragedy and others preceding it, much of the focus (and finger-pointing) has been about the warning signs that were reportedly missed or ignored. Parents and politicians alike have called for efforts to identify the would-be perpetrators—the "few bad apples" who are rotten to the core—before they wreak havoc on their classmates. However, some important lessons on the ABCs of prediction may increase the chances for success.

Predicting violent behavior, especially in rare and extreme forms, is enormously difficult. In terms of the "few bad apples" theory, there are lots of apples that are not quite perfect in color, size or shape, but are fine just beneath the skin. There are lots of kids who look, act, or dress like our image of the schoolyard shooter—they might wear black trench coats, scary tattoos, or gang headgear. Yet very few of them will translate their deviant adolescent attitudes into dangerous acts of violence. The few accurate predictions will be far outnumbered by the many "false positives."

Plus an attempt to single out the potential troublemakers could do more harm than good, by stigmatizing, marginalizing, and traumatizing already troubled youth. "Don't play with Johnnie—he's a bad apple." Already ostracized and picked on by his peers, Johnnie will now sense that even the teachers and the administration are against him. The "bad apple" label could even become a self-fulfilling prophecy, encouraging doubly-alienated children to act out violently.

Despite the limitations in predicting violence, a host of prediction tools have been widely disseminated in the wake of several episodes of school violence. The U.S. Department of Education sent to every public school in America a manual which highlights 16 warning signs of violence. This broad-ranging collection of red flags includes children who bully classmates as well as children who are bullied by their classmates. Another telltale sign warns of youngsters having low interest in academics. Just these three flags would capture significant shares of most middle school populations. In an attempt not to miss on one potential troublemaker, the net widens to include nearly everyone.

The American Psychological Association, in conjunction with MTV, also produced a handy pamphlet of warning signs which is now very much in demand. The National School Safety Center offers a similar checklist of 20 warning signs. School districts across America are distributing these pocket guides, hoping that teachers will determine how their students measure up on these scales of violence proneness. Even the FBI is getting into the act, beginning to train educators in the craft of profiling potentially violent students.

Stressing how to identify characteristics of the individual troublemaker lets schools off the hook. By turning the problem into a lesson in abnormal psychology, the blame can be located outside of the school setting—in a child's inadequate upbringing, in excessive exposure to violent media, in parental neglect and abuse (that is, bad apples not falling far from the tree). From this perspective, students have to change, not the schools.

Focusing on the individual child also ignores the fact that students often act far differently in group settings than when alone. To understand the course of events in Jonesboro and Littleton, for example, we must examine the relationships and interactions among the perpetrators as closely as we scrutinize their personal backgrounds and individual pathologies. To children, the expectations and approval of peers can be all important, especially when parents and other adults are not around. The issue may not be one of a few bad apples, but of a poorly tended orchard.

The best approach to reducing the potential for violence through prediction involves reducing the caseload of teachers and guidance counselors. Smaller classes and increased staffing would allow school personnel to observe even subtle issues, which cannot be easily determined from a simplistic checklist. More important, our focus should not be on the potentially violent kid, but on the unhappy kid (although at times these may be one and the same). We should use warning signs, but to reach troubled youngsters, long before they become troublesome. If we wait until a student has murderous intentions, we have waited much too long.

In whatever we do, we should borrow the physician's credo: Do no harm. With the help of school personnel (who often spend more time with children than even parents), we can make a difference. Perhaps we ought to develop warning signs to identify dangerous school environments rather than dangerous students, and then get to work improving the climate for learning and for living.

Filling the
After-School Wasteland

James Alan Fox published this opinion piece in the The Massachusetts
Exchange *(Winter 1998). Based on time-of-day patterns of juvenile
violence, he calls for the expanded use of after-school programs.*

For the past several years, I have advocated forcefully and repeatedly for the
expansion of after-school programs. Just a few weeks ago, at a Washington
press briefing held in cooperation with the Office of United States Attorney
General Janet Reno, I released a report promoting after-school initiatives as
a form of youth crime prevention. I have also testified on a number of occasions in the United States Congress and have lobbied White House policy
advisors—even meeting personally with President Clinton and Vice President Gore—about the need to invest in programs for children to fill the several hour void that starts when the school day ends.

At the national level, I have been able to grab the attention of many of
our political leaders with eye-opening statistics showing that the prime time
for juvenile crime is in the afternoon—after the school bell rings and before
many parents return home from work. The latest available data on time-of-
day for juvenile crime, based on offense reports from eight states, including
Massachusetts, shows that half of the juvenile violent offenses—assaults
and homicides—occur during the after-school hours when many children
are unsupervised and literally have too much free time to kill. By contrast,
relatively few juvenile crimes are committed after midnight when many
communities think they need curfews. It is also noteworthy that the incidence of teen violence spikes during the 3 o'clock hour, just as many youngsters escape from hours inside the confines of their school buildings into the
relative freedom of their neighborhoods.

Cities and towns across the Commonwealth of Massachusetts vary
considerably, of course, in the extent to which youth violence and gang
identification are recognized as local problems. The time-of-day patterns of
youth crime may, therefore, be of less significance for some communities
than others. Yet, the same concern for teen idleness and boredom in the

after-school wasteland directly affects other vital (and perhaps more universal) issues, such as teen drug and alcohol abuse as well as teen pregnancy.

A few weeks ago, I spoke to a parents-teachers organization in my own home town—a quiet and relatively crime-free bedroom community just south of Boston. I emphasized the need to support exciting after-school activities for youth—programs much more attractive than just group babysitting in an empty classroom. Although many in attendance were sympathetic and supportive, some townspeople simply felt that once the school bell rings the supervision of children ceases to be a public school matter.

Many citizens with whom I speak argue for a greater involvement and responsibility by parents—like in the "good old days" when it is said that parents took their role more seriously and unselfishly. Yet, many parents work long hours out of economic necessity. Others do so by choice, but who really can blame them? While some parents are ill-prepared or unmotivated for the critical and awesome task of raising their children, most parents are well-meaning and would like to have a greater role in the upbringing of their kids. Unfortunately, there are many more demands today on the time and attention of parents, just as there are many more distractions for children. Communities should assist parents, not assail them.

Responding to School Violence

*Jack Levin and Heather Beth Johnson co-authored an earlier version of
this essay for the* Boston Globe *(September 23, 1997). Based on a survey
of school administrators, they make specific recommendations about the
use of after-school programs in the fight against school violence.*

Notwithstanding several highly publicized cases of mass shootings at schools
around the country, the number of students murdered at school has recently plummeted. During the school year 1992–93, for example, there
were 44 murders at school; by the academic year 1998–99, that number had
dropped to 20 victims.

Many schools now offer a wide array of programs and activities aimed
at preventing or resolving violent student behavior. Conflict resolution programs are extremely popular in elementary, middle, and high schools. In
addition, especially in the high and middle schools, there are peer-media-
tion programs, programs to combat hatred and racism, and community volunteers to serve as tutors and mentors.

However, while after-school programs such as intramural athletics,
drama, art, music, and student government are offered by many high
schools and middle schools, very few elementary schools sponsor such programs. The concentration of such measures in the 6th through 12th grades
may result from the way in which principals differ by level as to how they
frame the problem of student violence. A majority of principals in charge of
elementary schools pinpoint the sources of student violence in factors exter-
nal to their schools. To these administrators, children are the victims of
family conflict, bad parenting, or excessive exposure to media violence. By
contrast, most of the high and middle school principals single out some
characteristics of the students themselves as being in need of change—gang
rivalries, inadequate academic preparation, racial hostility, rumors in the
hallway, or poor communication skills. These principals tend to regard their
high and middle school students not as victims of violence, but as its perpetrators. From this point of view, school programs are important for their
ability to change those student characteristics associated with violence and
conflict, whether idleness, hatred, or some form of incompetence.

Whatever the reason, the virtual absence of after-school activities in grades K through five leaves many younger children without opportunities for wholesome experiences and activities in the afternoons. Moreover, because they generally do not begin until the middle school years, supervised activities after school have not become part of the students' daily routine and therefore may not be seen as "cool" by the students who most need them. By the time such programs are available, students have already entered adolescence and may be unwilling to participate in activities supervised by adults, especially by their teachers and parents.

Although most urban high schools and middle schools provide at least some after-school activities, such programs are usually restricted to students who are in academic good standing, haven't been troublesome in the classroom, have economic resources, or can find transportation home. In most of the schools offering after-school activities, one or more restrictions are placed on the students' eligibility to participate. As a result, students most lacking in healthy alternatives after classes end—those who are impoverished, alienated, and idle—are literally left out in the cold.

According to school principals, a major reason why so many schools impose eligibility requirements for participating in after-school activities involves a lack of economic resources. Such programs are vastly under-funded.

But another reason has to do with the manner in which such activities are defined by the administrators themselves who fail to recognize after-school programs as violence or conflict prevention measures. They are much more likely to view such activities as a privilege extended to deserving students—those who are achievement-oriented, compliant, and well-behaved.

More than 40 percent of all violent crimes committed by teenagers occur in the late afternoon. Yet, today, 57 percent of all juveniles lack full-time parental supervision; they grow up in dual-career families or in single-parent households, where they are expected to fend for themselves after the school bell rings and they are dismissed for the day.

In wealthy communities, many children may be provided with opportunities for healthy after-school alternatives. In areas where economic and human resources are seriously lacking, however, children tend to be on their own until their parents come home from work.

Therefore, expanding the school day to include all students in after-school programs would structure our youngsters' days so that their time could be spent on worthwhile activities. Actually, what we currently regard as after-school programs should be incorporated into a longer school day during which traditional academics become interspersed among clubs, internships, athletic programs, job apprenticeships, and the arts. By re-structuring the school experience so that it is identified with more than academic subjects, the meaning of school would be broadened to include appealing and practical activities from the youngsters' standpoint.

Such an approach requires making a major investment—one that ought to be shared by a wide range of local interests and institutions. The cost would be heavy, but not nearly so heavy in human terms as our continuing disinvestment in our children and their future. Some 135,000 U.S. teenagers go to school each day carrying a firearm. It would be a step in the right direction if they traded in their weapons for softball gloves, tennis rackets, and art supplies.

A Failing Grade in Response to Columbine

We prepared this essay for the one-year anniversary of the Columbine shooting. Published in the Dallas Morning News *(April 16, 2000), the column assesses progress that was made in the wake of this tragedy.*

It has been a year since two students at Columbine High School in Littleton, Colo. opened fire on their classmates and teachers, perpetrating the bloodiest school shooting in American history.

In the aftermath of the massacre, Americans were horrified. Across the country, groups of anxious parents, teachers, and psychologists huddled in seminars, conferences, and meetings to address the issue of students who seek to get even with a semiautomatic weapon.

Only now do we realize exactly what lessons Americans have learned from the experience of mass murder at Columbine High on April 20, 1999. Judging by the policies and practices implemented during the past year, it is sad to say they have learned absolutely nothing.

In many middle and high schools, principals have installed metal detectors, stationed armed officers at entrances and fitted hallways with surveillance cameras (even if they couldn't afford to hire the personnel to monitor them). Other schools have banned knapsacks that could hide a weapon deep within.

School boards also have instituted zero-tolerance policies, automatically suspending any student caught carrying a gun or threatening to blow up the school. Meanwhile, teachers have been handed manuals on the "warning signs" of violence and trained to spot troublemakers who have the potential of becoming the next schoolyard sniper.

Rather than employ long-term policies and programs that have some chance of reducing school violence, authorities have proposed short-term, politically expedient solutions.

School administrators typically have taken a law enforcement approach that, from the outset, had little if any chance to be effective but that was punitive enough to satisfy public opinion and pacify nervous parents.

They have spent millions of dollars on security equipment—money that could have been used to make genuine inroads in the battle against school violence and to upgrade the entire educational experience.

Even worse, panic-stricken school officials have suspended many students for the most trivial of reasons—from threatening to hurt Barney the purple dinosaur to making a gun out of construction paper. Students have been summarily expelled without regard to their unique circumstances or criminal history; classes have been canceled at the slightest provocation; and common sense has been ignored.

So, one year later, virtually all of the conditions that precipitated the Littleton massacre—and school shootings elsewhere—remain very much in place.

As much as ever, bullying is a daily threat to hundreds of thousands of youngsters, as cliques and intolerance for diversity continue to dominate school culture. Many children still attend schools that are far too populous and impersonal, and they sit in crowded classrooms where teachers simply are overwhelmed by the class size. Children are advised by overburdened psychologists, nurses, and guidance counselors who are lucky if they recognize the faces of their students, let alone their names and personal problems.

Cities and towns across the nation have begun to punish parents, through fines and even jail terms, when their children are truant from classes. Meanwhile, little attention has been devoted to finding ways of encouraging bored youngsters to attend school. The back-to-basics movement in public education has deprived many children of the "frills" that had made school halfway tolerable as well as esteem-building.

Students lack a sufficient range of extracurricular activities—from freshman sports teams to drama and chess clubs—which often were eliminated as cost-cutting measures. Wanting to feel special and to belong to something important, students instead may join other bored teens during the after-school hours, far away from the watchful guidance of adults, to celebrate the hate-filled ideology of Adolf Hitler or the mean-spirited teachings of the occult.

Too often, public opinion and criminal justice policy are shaped by collective hysteria in reaction to extraordinary events like Columbine. For example, many school officials respond to bullying only out of fear that some harassed high school student might decide to kill his classmates, not because it is the right thing to do or because it might improve the quality of life for all children. The problem with being scared into addressing an issue is that attention to it remains only so long as the perceived threat persists.

After just one year, Columbine seems like old news for many Americans. They since have moved on to address other seemingly more pressing issues—the skyrocketing price of gasoline or the plight of Elian Gonzalez—without ever having made effective changes in the conditions under which children go to school.

Regrettably, the legacy of the Columbine tragedy appears to be little more than a long list of ineffective quick fixes. In the midst of hype and hysteria, we never really came close to fixing the fundamental problems that alienate children. Despite the "A" for effort, America's campaign against school violence deserves a failing grade.

PART IV

RAMPAGE

When Misery Has No Company

Focusing on Mark Barton's Atlanta shooting spree, we published this analysis of mass murder in the Boston Globe *(August 7, 1999).*

In the aftermath of mass murder, everyone seems to have an opinion about the causes and cures. Eager to explain Mark Barton's slaughter of 12 people in Atlanta last week, some observers have blamed semiautomatic firearms and pushed for tighter gun controls; others have faulted day-trading as a high-risk form of gambling and proposed controls on this new style of investing.

Virtually no one, however, seems to have examined the fact that Barton, like so many other Americans nowadays, was socially isolated, lacking the support systems that might have gotten him through bad times and averted his devastating rampage.

Failure to recognize this growing defect within our social environment is like ignoring the link between skin cancer and the destruction of the ozone layer. Surely we can apply sun screen, wear protective clothing, even stay indoors and away from the sun, but without an effort to care for the physical environment, we may all be doomed.

The proliferation of high-powered firearms has undoubtedly contributed to the enormousness of the carnage in recent mass killings, but hardly determines whether a massacre will occur. Barton's first three victims—his wife and two children—were bludgeoned to death with a hammer, not shot. Lacking a semiautomatic, he could still have managed to stab or pummel to death at least a few of the stock traders against whom he sought revenge. Armed with only a knife or hammer, Barton's body count would have been smaller but still unacceptably high.

In almost every mass murder, the killer suffers a loss that from his point of view is catastrophic—typically the loss of a job or a relationship. Barton had recently dropped more than $100,000 in the stock market and was separated from his wife.

Like most other mass killers, Barton was a loner. At home he worked independently as a consultant and traded stocks on the Internet. Living apart from his wife and extended kin, he lacked the friends and family who might have given him the support and encouragement he so desperately needed. By last April Barton's losses were climbing fast—so fast that he forfeited his rental home and was forced to move back in with his estranged wife. Characteristically, he kept his miseries to himself.

Aside from the gunman, the real culprit in explaining mass murder can be found in society itself and in a trend that has affected almost everyone. During recent years, there has been an eclipse of community, a dwindling of the social relationships—family ties and neighborliness—that had protected former generations of Americans from succumbing to disaster.

In an earlier era, family or neighbors could be counted on to assist in times of financial ruin; today you're basically on your own. Many Americans simply have no place to turn when they get into trouble. Without options and without support, mass murder can sometimes seem like the only way out.

At the same time, growing numbers of Americans are opting for the solitude of telecommuting and the Internet. They avoid traffic jams on the highways but also give up interaction with co-workers. Their neighborhoods no longer provide them with a source of friendship and camaraderie. More typically, Americans don't even know their neighbors' names and faces—only the e-mail addresses of far-away acquaintances whom they have never met. We are quick to communicate at a superficial level with total strangers in chat rooms but too busy to sit with our neighbors and share a beer and conversation.

According to our data, areas of the country with large numbers of transients, newcomers, and drifters also have more than their share of mass killings. Boom cities with low unemployment and good weather are attractive to those who are looking for a new beginning or a last resort.

So long as these people remain in Omaha, Rochester, or Boston, they can depend on their families, friends, and fraternal organizations for personal assistance. But when they reach Los Angeles, Houston, or Atlanta, they find themselves very much alone. When times get tough, they have nobody around to discourage them from doing the wrong thing.

So before we attempt to ban all instruments of mass destruction, perhaps we should limit ways in which technology and mobility are slowly destroying our social fabric. Perhaps we should seek to repair the ozone layer in our social environment. For too many Americans who suffer, their misery has no company.

Termination Can Be Murder

In this assessment of workplace murder, published in the Boston Sunday Globe *(May 2, 1993), we present a profile of the disgruntled worker and identify the factors that encourage him to go on a rampage.*

Paul Calden said he'd be coming back...and he was true to his word. On January 27, 1993, eight months after being fired from his job at Fireman's Fund Insurance in Tampa, Florida, he returned to get even. This time, *he'd* be the one to do the firing. Calden approached three of his former supervisors as they were having lunch in the company cafeteria. Taking aim, he announced, "This is what you get for firing me," and calmly started shooting. By the time it was all over, Calden had killed his three managers and had wounded two other employees. His next and final victim was himself.

Calden's deadly rampage unnerved corporate executives from coast to coast. During the following two week period, four more disgruntled employees got their revenge for alleged unfair treatment, making workers in businesses large and small concerned about their personal safety.

The events of late January and early February 1993 highlight a growing and disturbing trend in America. In fact, based on available FBI data, the incidence of employees killing their supervisors has doubled over the last decade. At present, at least two cases occur each month in the United States. And the problem of workplace murder—committed by insiders rather than intruders—is likely to escalate in the years ahead.

For every disgruntled worker who attempts to get even through murder, there are countless others who make threats against the lives of their managers or, alternatively, sabotage company property or image. What kind of person contemplates solving his employment troubles through violence? What is the profile of the worker who decides to take out his frustrations on the boss—if not on the whole company?

The vengeful worker is typically a middle-aged white male who faces termination in a worsening economy. He sees little opportunity for finding another job, and suspects that all the breaks are going to younger competitors—or even to blacks, women, and foreigners. Having grown up in the Fifties and Sixties, an era of unparalleled prosperity, he feels entitled to a well-paying, meaningful job. Rudely awakened from the American Dream, he resents that his "birthright" has been snatched from him and looks for someone to blame.

Rarely will a younger worker respond so desperately to a termination. For him, it's the loss of a job, not a career—merely a temporary setback along the road to the success that he expects ultimately to achieve. A 20-year-old may respond to his firing by saying, "Take this job and shove it." By contrast, a 40-year-old feels shoved out by his job. At this juncture, the middle-aged man expects to be at the top of his career, not hitting rock bottom.

Demographic changes are exacerbating the effects of a post-industrial economy in which desirable middle-income jobs are becoming increasingly scarce. The baby boomers—76 million strong—are now in their 30s and 40s. For many of them, youthful enthusiasm has been shattered and replaced by anxiety concerning their financial well-being and a growing sense of resentment.

Some vengeful workers have suffered repeated failures in their careers, resulting in a diminished ability to cope with life's disappointments. From their point of view, they never get the right job, the deserved promotion, a decent raise. Their firing at a crucial time in their lives becomes the final straw.

Others may have come to feel invulnerable to job loss because of their long-term employment with the same company. From their perspective, they have given their best years to the boss, have unselfishly dedicated their careers to the firm, have helped build the business...and what do they get in return? Fired!

Of course, most disgruntled employees and ex-employees don't take out their anger on the company. Some may blame themselves, become depressed, and consider suicide as their only option. Others may take out their frustrations on their family. But for the one who typically externalizes blame, responsibility always lies elsewhere. "It's not my fault," he reasons, "The boss doesn't give me good assignments, my supervisor doesn't appreciate my work, and the guy at the next desk keeps taking credit for my accomplishments." When cited for poor work performance, he lashes out at those he holds accountable for his failures. While worker grievances are often legitimate, in this age of diminished individual responsibility, more and more workers refuse to accept blame for their own incompetence.

Even disgruntled employees who hold their bosses responsible may not resort to violence, especially if they enjoy strong support systems—such as family and friends—to help get them through the tough times. Those who do become violent tend to be loners. They may live by themselves, have recently separated or divorced, or have moved thousands of miles from home. Socially isolated, they regard work as the only meaningful part of their lives. When they lose their job, they lose everything.

Here too we see a trend in society which places more and more middle-aged men at risk. An increased rate of divorce, greater residential mobility, and a general lack of neighborliness mean that, for many Americans, work is their *only* source of stability and companionship.

In a shrinking job market, who can blame an employee for devoting all of his time and energy to his career, even though it might jeopardize his marriage and home life, not to mention his health? Seeking a competitive edge, many companies encourage, if not require, their employees to work long hours. In fact, those employees who are fortunate enough to survive layoffs are often expected to take up the slack through overtime.

It is up to companies, therefore, to endeavor to reverse this dangerous and unhealthful trend. A single-minded focus on financial profit and loss ignores the human dimension.

Last week, Attorney General Janet Reno told Department of Justice employees that she hoped "to develop new attitudes and programs that will enable people to achieve their professional goals while having the opportunity to spend quality time with their families." Taking this cue, employers should encourage workers to maintain balance in their lives, to make ample time for family, friends, and hobbies. Work should be important and meaningful, but not everything.

Even enlightened companies may be forced to terminate employees, either because of financial exigencies or worker incompetence. Unfortunately, many businesses do not invest as much time and effort in firing as they do in hiring. Rather than take a proactive approach in their procedures for termination and layoffs, they ignore the potential for employee violence…unless, of course, a threat has been made.

In this connection, employers often do not fully recognize the importance of human resources personnel, because these specialists are not directly involved with income-production. After all, they don't make the widgets, sell the widgets, or distribute the widgets. Ironically, companies facing layoffs will often first make cuts in their human resources departments under a misguided logic: The human resources department is not needed because the company isn't hiring anymore. Yet these are the very employees who are best able to deal with potentially vengeful workers.

With the assistance of human resources specialists, terminated employees should be treated with compassion and aided in making the transition to another job through aggressive and humane outplacement efforts. Even when terminating someone, an employer should strive to provide the very kind of support that may be missing in the lives of the most volatile employees.

Workplace morale is not the only thing at stake. An embittered and obsessed worker can come close to destroying a company through sabotage or violence. A company that takes seriously its humanitarian obligations to employees may not only minimize workplace burnout, but also prevent a workplace shoot-out.

American Workplace
Needs Humanizing

In this essay prepared for the Christian Science Monitor
*(March 23, 1998), we suggest measures that can be adopted
by businesses to reduce the threat of lethal violence*

This month, a reportedly deranged man—back to work at the Connecticut State Lottery following a stress-related leave—went on a deadly rampage, killing four of his superiors before turning the gun on himself.

The details seemed all too familiar. The gunman was 35-year-old Matthew Beck, who had accused his employer of treating him badly. He'd complained that his supervisors were stalling on negotiations to pay him back wages and that he was not being assigned any work. Months earlier, he'd filed a grievance contending that he was being assigned jobs outside of his work classification and that he deserved a raise of $2 an hour. Just a few days before his rampage, he spoke angrily of suing the Lottery.

For the American worker, the past ten years haven't been completely kind. Although unemployment has dropped to below 5 percent, underemployment is increasingly the norm, with many middle-income, manufacturing jobs being replaced by lower-paying positions in the service industry. More and more workers have been forced to take temporary or part-time jobs without fringe benefits.

In response to cut-throat competition, some unhappy workers have simply given up on themselves. Others have sought legal remedies. But more and more, embittered, vengeful workers have settled matters outside of court—with fighting words and a loaded gun. To many casual observers, the problem of workplace violence is often equated with disgruntled postal workers. The term "going postal" has become a code word for workplace massacres, and there is even a new computer game, simply called "Postal," with the theme of going berserk in public places. As the Connecticut incident indicates, the problem of workplace violence extends well beyond the confines of local postal facilities.

Nationally, about four people are murdered every month at the hands of a co-worker or former co-worker. And for every incident of workplace homicide, thousands of workers are assaulted or threatened by an associate. Less conspicuous are the countless numbers of angry workers who seek to sabotage their company's bottom line by spreading ugly rumors to hurt sales or subverting the manufacturing process.

In response to rising levels of workplace violence, a wide range of books and pamphlets, seminars, and consultants have surfaced to help companies cope with the growing threat of violence on the job. Some experts focus on security concerns, others on promoting effective screening techniques or channels of communications to alert management to troublesome workers.

The overriding goal should be to make civility and decency in the workplace as critical as profit. Companies need to upgrade and humanize the way in which they deal with all employees every day rather than just to focus narrowly on how to respond to the one who has made threats. Long-term planning to improve employee morale pays off in human terms. A study conducted for Northwestern National Life Insurance concluded that companies with effective grievance, harassment, and security procedures also reported lower rates of workplace violence.

Twenty or 30 years ago, the bond between management and worker was stronger. But loyalty between worker and boss has gone the way of the dinosaur, replaced with an adversarial perspective on both sides. Moreover, the problem of workplace violence is broader than just the disgruntled worker. To a greater extent, customers and clients in hospitals, law firms, and other public and private worksites are expressing their displeasure in the most explosive way. Here too, rather than seeking to become more people-minded, corporate America seems to be moving in the wrong direction. As a result, disgruntled clients and customers confront frustrating automated phone systems as well as poorly-trained and uninspired customer relations staff.

In today's corporate environment, it is increasingly difficult to find someone in charge who has the ability, the authority, and the desire to make things right. Apparently, these days even the customer is not always right, unless, of course, he is packing an AK47.

Postal Violence: Cycle of Despair Turns Tragic

Because of a series of massacres in post offices around the country, the term going postal became a code word for workplace murder generally. In this column for USA Today *(May 12, 1993), we describe the conditions that made the United States Postal Service particularly vulnerable to this type of violence.*

Violence is fast becoming as much a tradition at the post office as Bermuda shorts and special delivery. In the past decade alone, there have been 11 shootings at U.S. postal facilities, tragically claiming the lives of 31 postal workers.

What made the two most recent incidents especially shocking was that they occurred on the same day—"Black Thursday"—last week. Just before 9 A.M., 45-year-old postal employee Larry Jasion walked into the Dearborn, Mich., postal garage and calmly opened fire on his supervisor and co-workers before taking his own life. Four hours later, 39-year-old former letter carrier Mark Richard Hilbun burst into the post office at Dana Point, Calif., allegedly shooting two postal workers and then fleeing in the mass confusion.

What exactly is going on in the Postal Service? America wants to know, and so does Congress.

Actually, to some extent post office violence reflects a growing trend in workplace murder by disgruntled employees at all kinds of job sites—at least two per month in the United States. More than ever, embittered workers are taking matters—and guns—into their own hands and are getting even with bosses whom they blame for their problems on the job. In their way of thinking, "Look who's doing the firing now!"

But the Postal Service still has had more than its share of violence, about seven times as many incidents of murder as would be expected of its three-quarter-million employees.

Growing numbers of postal workers complain that management is arbitrary and autocratic, and they express deep concern about job security in the face of automation and reorganization. What hope does a fired middle-age letter carrier have of finding an equivalent job given his years of experi-

50

ence walking around the neighborhood with a leather bag slung over his shoulder?

Even his specialized skill in sorting mail has little market value. Indeed, his only option might be a minimum-wage job, selling cigarettes at the local convenience store or working in a company mail room.

To top it all off, postal workers typically get no respect from the public, which blames them when the mail is late or even when the price of a stamp goes up a penny.

In addition, some postal workers feel a strong sense of entitlement—because of their long-term employment, civil service status and "veterans preference." From their perspective, they have given their best years to the Postal Service—and what do they get in return? Fired!

Little wonder that those who are laid off, threatened with termination or denied a promotion respond with such resentment and despair.

Of course, most of them don't take out their anger on the post office. Some may blame themselves, become depressed or consider suicide as their only option. Others may take out their frustrations on their families. But for the one who typically externalizes blame, responsibility always lies elsewhere. "It's not my fault," he reasons. "My supervisor doesn't give me good assignments and refuses to appreciate my hard work."

It will undoubtedly take a long-term effort—more than just a task force or a congressional investigation—to reverse the culture of violence among postal workers. As a positive step, Postmaster General Marvin Runyon has indicated his desire to abandon the longstanding quasi-military management style about which postal workers often complain.

Beyond softening the hierarchy of authority in day-to-day employee relations, the Postal Service desperately needs to take a more humane approach to terminations and downsizing. This should involve aggressive human resources strategies for dealing with employees who are, for whatever reason, removed from the job. Both management and workers must share responsibility for helping less fortunate co-workers make the transition to other employment.

A decade of violence has created new and frightening options for resolving work-related disputes. In the thoughts of vengeful postal workers around the country are the names of their infamous colleagues who have evened the score through murder. If the cycle of hopelessness and despair is allowed to continue, more disgruntled postal workers and ex-postal workers will follow the lead of those who have made revenge a Postal Service tradition.

Placing the Blame
for the Palm Bay Massacre

In this opinion piece written for the Orlando Sentinel *(May 3, 1987),
we criticize the tendency to look for easy scapegoats in the aftermath
of a violent rampage.*

While the families of the six slain victims mourn in the aftermath of the Palm Bay shooting, others are looking to place the blame. It seems to us that they are looking in the wrong place. Rather than focusing their anger on the sniper himself or even on our absurdly liberal gun laws, some residents of Palm Bay criticize the local police force.

Neighbors claim that they had frequently called the police to complain about the alleged murderer's bizarre behavior. He scared away neighborhood children who annoyed him by waving his gun in the air in a threatening way. "Why wasn't anything done before six innocent people were shot down in cold blood?" Residents are demanding an answer.

The tendency to look for a convenient scapegoat in the face of such senseless tragedy is both understandable and common, even if unfair. In 1966, Charles Whitman's psychiatrist was bitterly criticized for having done nothing when his patient related his secret fantasy to climb the tower at the University of Texas and shoot people. Days later, Whitman killed 14.

In 1984, James Huberty's wife was blamed by the residents of San Ysidro, Cal., for not having stopped her husband when he said he was going hunting for humans. Moments later, James Huberty gunned down 21 in the local McDonald's. Most unfair of all, management was held responsible by many postal workers for Pat Sherrill's 1986 massacre of 14 employees at the Edmond, Oklahoma, post office.

Unfortunately, there is little anyone could have done to prevent these mass murders. Hindsight is always 20/20; after the fact, one can always find warning signals that had been present, but were less obvious before a tragedy occurred.

But to see them ahead of time and to be able to prevent what eventually did happen is quite another thing. It is simply impossible to predict mass murder before it occurs. Most people who act bizarrely, whose behavior seems inappropriate, who behave unneighborly, or even who threaten others will never kill anyone. Moreover, unless a crime has been committed, nothing substantial can be done anyway. Unneighborliness is hardly a criminal offense, at least not yet.

Applying our point of view to the Palm Bay massacre emphasizes the futility of efforts to prevent such crimes. Precisely what would the residents of Palm Bay have wanted the police to do with William Cruse in response to his obnoxious actions toward his neighbors? Would an official warning have forestalled his angry outburst? Or, would it have precipitated it? Should he have been arrested? If so, for what? Should Cruse have been jailed for waving a gun in the air in a threatening manner? If so, for how long? What would really have been accomplished once he was released a short time later?

We fear that some people might answer many of these questions in the affirmative. They would have the police arrest all social misfits and either imprison them or coerce them into treatment. It wouldn't matter if they had never committed a crime, only that their behavior was eccentric. We would get them all, all thousands of them, in a massive nationwide roundup. In the process, we would perhaps reduce the number of mass murders that occur in the country, but we would also have reduced our republic to the state of an armed dictatorship.

Mass murder is an American phenomenon; so too is our love affair with weapons of mass destruction such as handguns and rifles. Rather than rounding up people, let's try rounding up the weapons that make such crimes a reality.

PART V

HATE HOMICIDE

Hatred: Too Close for Comfort

Published in the St. Petersburg Times *(July 13, 1993), Jack Levin describes the perils associated with studying a phenomenon that makes people feel uncomfortable, if not personally threatened.*

For the past decade, I have studied serial and mass killers. In the course of conducting research, I have interviewed them, consulted with their attorneys, talked with their wives and mothers, and written about them.

During this entire period, my ideas about murder were generally well-received. In fact, many people apparently found them fascinating; so fascinating that the book I co-authored a few years ago, *Mass Murder: America's Growing Menace,* sold more than 50,000 copies and got me on national television talk shows from *Geraldo* to *Oprah,* from *48 Hours* to *Unsolved Mysteries.* Even *Saturday Night Live,* in a skit about Jeffrey Dahmer's trial, alluded to my work. In all candor, I began to feel like a celebrity.

Sure, there was an occasional death threat (for example, from a fan of Charlie Manson) and a few nasty phone calls. But the overwhelming response was quite positive. Even the serial killers didn't seem to mind. One Canadian killer I got to know used to call me from his prison cell every Tuesday (collect, of course) and was very cooperative in responding to my students' letters to him about serial murder. He must have been flattered by the attention.

Then, a couple of years ago, I began to notice that racial conflagrations in the major cities of the United States were becoming more commonplace. Believing that a national crisis was at hand, I began to research the rising tide of bigotry in America in the form of hate crimes—offenses committed against individuals because of their race, religion, national origin, or sexual orientation. In my talks and lectures to students, I pointed out that only 5 percent of such crimes are perpetrated by members of organized groups like the Klan or the White Aryan Resistance. Most are committed by otherwise ordinary citizens—teenagers down the block, the guy at the next desk at work, or the neighbors next door. I emphasized also that I was not talking about first amendment, free speech issues such as whether or not it is legal to insult someone with a racial slur. Actually, half of all hate crimes reported to the police are nothing less than assaults, often brutal attacks that put their victims in the hospital. I noted that African-Americans are most often victimized, but that gay men are most likely to suffer severe injuries as a result of an attack against them.

All of a sudden, I was no longer regarded as fascinating. On the contrary, people seemed uncomfortable, upset, even angered, by what I had to say. I got the strong feeling that I was perceived as a personal threat, as someone who stirs up trouble and delves into matters better left unsaid. In response to a talk I had given on campus, for example, a student wrote an angry letter to the editor of the school newspaper, in which he defended the most racist ideas and referred to me as a "left-wing fascist." I later determined that he had not even attended my lecture, but had used the topic of my speech as an excuse to vent his anger.

The pattern was now obvious. By shifting my attention from serial killers to the perpetrators of hate crimes, I had turned away from *them* and toward *us*. Serial murder is so extraordinary that, for the average American, it might as well be fiction. The topic of hate crimes, by contrast, is real; it simply hits too close to home.

The particularly enlightened host of a local radio talk show in Boston recently asked me to be on her show. For more than an hour, I was scolded, reprimanded, and castigated in phone calls from her listeners. First, I talked with an outraged German-American man who claimed that recent acts of violence against immigrants in German cities had been grossly exaggerated. He blamed the "media." I agreed with him that relatively few radical skinheads had been directly responsible for the violence in Germany, but I also pointed out that 15 percent of German youths said that they now consider Adolph Hitler to be a great man and up to 40 percent of all German citizens express some sympathy for issues of "racial purity" and "Germany for Germans." I also emphasized that violence against foreigners was not a German predicament exclusively, but a world-wide problem. The next caller was a Rush Limbaugh fan who was furious because I had criticized his conservative idol for belittling gay activists and for referring to women as "Femi-Nazis." I tried to explain that Rush was probably a very nice guy, but that his name-calling may be misinterpreted by naive youngsters looking to justify their bashings of women and gays. Next, I heard from a Jewish man from

Framingham, Massachusetts who was angry because I hadn't mentioned black anti-Semitism. I suggested to him that hatred can be found on all sides of the race issue, but that vulnerable people everywhere—blacks, Jews, Latinos, Asians, gays, and the disabled—should put aside their differences to form a powerful coalition against bigotry. He wasn't convinced. My final call was from a white supremacist in New Hampshire who claimed that Jews control the government, the banks, and the media and that black-Americans would be better off if they all went back to Africa. I should have calmly retorted that Jews probably do control the delis in New York City but that they are vastly under-represented among bank executives. Or, I should have pointed out that the average income of Irish-Americans is almost identical to that of Jews, yet Irish-Americans are never accused of controlling anything except the bars and the local police force (a stereotype no less absurd). I should have told the white supremacist that the ancestors of most black-Americans have probably been in this country longer than any of his relatives...Maybe he should be the one to pack his bags. Before I could respond, however, the white racist had hung up and the program was over. The experience left me totally depressed.

Hardly a day passes without some grotesque hate crime being reported in the local newspapers; and I am convinced more than ever that our nation is in serious trouble, that we could easily be torn apart in the next few years by the growing presence of hatred. Coming to grips with bigotry and violence might well be central to our survival as a free society into the next century. Yet Americans don't seem to be willing to address the problem, even if it is spiraling out of control. Perhaps they prefer watching escapist fare like *The Silence of the Lambs* or *The Texas Chainsaw Massacre*. Maybe I should go back to studying something safer...like serial killers.

Is American Culture to Blame for the Oklahoma Tragedy?

In this essay written for the Boston Globe *(April 27, 1995), Jack Levin and Jack McDevitt observe that hatemongers often derive their inspiration from mainstream leaders.*

The bloodiest violence is often facilitated by messages of bias and bigotry. In the area of hate crimes, the most hideous offenses are frequently committed by fringe members of hate groups who hear the repeated rhetoric of their racist leaders as some sort of signal exhorting them to go out and kill or injure in order to demonstrate their commitment to the "cause." While it is too early to know all that happened in Oklahoma City, preliminary evidence strongly suggests a similar pattern where marginal members of a local para-military group were responsible for the most brutal act of domestic terrorism in American history.

Unfortunately, it isn't only the irrational leaders of a few extremist right-wing organizations who are sending messages of intolerance. Even our mainstream leaders seem to be caught up in the public expression of nastiness.

Senator D'Amato recently infuriated the Japanese-American community by caricaturing, in a mocking rendition of a Japanese accent, Judge Lance Ito's Asian heritage.

Shock jock Howard Stern poked fun at the murder of popular singer Selena and accused her Latino fans of having bad taste.

O.J. Simpson lawyer Robert Shapiro handed out fortune cookies after the relentless cross-examination of a Chinese-American criminalist.

Representative Richard Armey "mistakenly" referred to a gay congressional colleague as "Barney Fag."

Khalid Mohammed, a spokesman for the Nation of Islam, told college students in New Jersey that Jews were "people of the Devil."

Discussing the terrorist bombing in Oklahoma City, a popular local talk show host referred to Arabs as "towel people."

When so many influential mainstream leaders—politicians, talk-show hosts, educators and attorneys—cavalierly make stereotyped statements in public, you begin to realize that their insensitive remarks express more than just individual prejudices. If it ever existed at all, political correctness is now dead and buried and has been replaced by a mean-spirited culture of hate and violence, in which vulnerable people are routinely disparaged, belittled, and insulted. What used to be whispered behind closed doors about blacks, Jews, Asians, Arabs, Latinos, women, or gays is now openly flaunted among total strangers without fear of reprimand or retaliation. What in former times might have been regarded as an illegitimate means of protest is now being embraced by growing numbers of resentful, angry and often hate-filled Americans.

The stereotyped thinking that seems so fashionable nowadays, even in the most respectable circles, has its counterpart in the racist ideology of the radical far-right. Its white supremacist leaders talk in code words and phrases about the same issues that concern middle America. They preach that the heritage of white Christians is being eroded by foreign (meaning: Jewish) influence; they lament the rise of government interference (meaning: Jews in high places who have forced racial integration and affirmative action down the throats of white Americans); and they condemn welfare cheating (meaning: blacks). At Sunday services, dedicated members of the movement listen intently as their Identity Church preachers claim that white Anglo-Saxons are the true Israelites depicted in the Old Testament, while Jews are really the children of Satan. Members of the congregation nod in agreement as their leaders declare that all blacks, Asians, and Latinos are "mud people" at the same spiritual level as animals and therefore have no souls. After services, husbands, fathers, and brothers all adjourn to the woods for their weekly military maneuvers. Clad in battle fatigues and carrying their assault rifles over their shoulders, they rally against the federal government, the imaginary enemy that they refer to as Zionist Occupied (Z.O.G.).

The culture of hate is deeply implicated in the growing incidence of hate crimes—brutal attacks directed against individuals simply because they are different in terms of their race, religion, gender, or sexual orientation. For example, Klanwatch notes a 26 percent increase in bias motivated assaults between 1993 and 1994. For the same 12-month period, the Anti-Defamation League reports a 10 percent increase in anti-Jewish incidents. Not coincidentally, the Southern Poverty Law Center also concludes that organized hate groups staged an "alarming comeback" in 1994.

The same kind of stereotyped thinking that has recently invaded the mainstream of American culture has also made it possible for anti-government extremists to justify their evil deeds. It is a safe bet that those individuals responsible for blowing up the Federal Building in Oklahoma City saw their actions as attacking only "the enemy," i.e., the federal government. They probably didn't envision children playing in a daycare center, out-of-work men and women receiving their unemployment checks, or local residents picking up their mail. They wouldn't have been interested in understanding the profound emotional impact on the family members and friends of the innocent victims of their terrorist attack.

The growing presence of a culture of hate reminds us that hate crimes are only the tip of the iceberg of bigotry and prejudice. Popular culture often represents a more pervasive, if less extreme, version of the same underlying hostilities that trigger terrorist behavior. There are many Americans who are very angry—if not quite angry enough to vandalize a cemetery, assault someone whose skin color is different, or blow up a federal building. Instead, they might only parrot the racist remarks of their favorite politician, shout their agreement with a racist talk show host, or laugh at a racist stand-up comic. For a few misguided souls, however, the culture of hate is simply not enough to satisfy their need for malice, their quest for personal justice. They decide to go beyond the words of Representative Armey, Senator D'Amato, and Howard Stern.

German Violence: Are We Next?

In this essay published in the Chicago Tribune *(May 4, 1993), Jack Levin and Jack McDevitt argue that the same forces responsible for the increase in hate violence in Germany may be found in American society as well.*

The voices of xenophobia and racism are once again being raised around the world. A mob of neo-Nazi youths recently rampaged through neighborhood streets, hurling bottles and rocks, smashing cars and homes, and shouting "Kill the Jews." In a separate incident, eight young men were charged in the brutal murder of a 19-year-old foreigner who was thrown to the ground and kicked to death. Skinheads in a medium-sized industrial city threatened local school teachers with a loaded .357 Magnum and etched the words "No Jews," "Happy Birthday Hitler," and "Jew bitch," along with S.S. symbols and swastikas into classroom doors. The windows of an Islamic Mosque were shattered and its Moslem worshipers were threatened with gunfire.

Actually, none of these shocking incidents occurred in countries like Germany or Bosnia. All of them were recently committed in the United States—in Crown Heights, New York; Coral Springs, Florida; Glendale, California; and Dayton, Ohio—by American youngsters. As we shake our heads in dismay at brutal group confrontations in Europe, hundreds of racial and ethnic attacks occur in the United States.

The intensity of racial and ethnic animosity in the United States cannot yet compare with that in some European countries. In certain German cities, for example, the unemployment rate has reached 40 percent and hundreds of thousands of political refugees continue to flow into the country.

Yet many of the same factors operating to produce German racism are at work in the United States as well. Growing numbers of Americans feel personally threatened by the presence of newcomers and minorities who compete for diminishing amounts of wealth, status, and power. In fact, they are being challenged, to an increasing extent, by a broad range of "outsiders." The growing presence of women, people of color, and international students has threatened the dominance of white males on college campuses across the country. More and more lesbians and gay men have expressed their demands in assertive public demonstrations including, most recently, to be accepted

61

into America's military. And, affirmative action guidelines are widely regarded as "reverse discrimination" policies which, at the expense of white males, grant special treatment to "undeserving" minorities and women.

What is more, we are currently in the midst of possibly the largest wave of immigration in U.S. history. Between 1981 and 1990, more than 7 million newcomers left their homelands to begin new lives in America. There will be more newcomers in the United States in the 1990s than in any previous decade; and the overwhelming majority are Asians, Latinos, and blacks.

Within the lifetime of most Americans living today, the white Anglo-Saxon majority will have become a statistical minority—in fact, in many American cities, this has already occurred. People of color—Asians, Latinos, and blacks—will increasingly challenge the traditional power structure; they will more and more be demanding to share the wealth of the nation. In our post-industrial society, there is likely to be growing conflict among groups for scarce economic resources.

Large-scale racial violence has already erupted in our major cities. Since 1980, there have been racial confrontations in Los Angeles, New York City, Miami, Washington D.C., Detroit, and Newark. Additionally, the Southern Poverty Law Center has recently documented an unprecedented number of hate-motivated murders across the United States.

Throughout the country, laws prohibiting hate crimes are being strengthened and local prosecutors and judges are beginning to be more responsive to the victims of hate violence. Yet, in terms of embracing all victims of bias-motivated crime and providing appropriate sentencing, change continues to be very slow and uneven. Some groups in need of protection, for example, women and gays, are left out of many state statutes, and offenders are too often permitted to go free with a slap on the wrist.

Most frightening is the potential retreat by the Supreme Court from its role as a protector of civil rights. In April, the Court heard oral arguments in the case of the State of Wisconsin versus Todd Mitchell concerning the constitutionality of statutes which increase the penalty for hate crimes based on race, religion, disability, sexual orientation, or national origin. Hate attacks are nothing less than acts of domestic terrorism—they are intended to send a message not only to the victim but to all members of the victim's group: "Move into this neighborhood, attend this school, or work in this company, and the same thing will happen to you." The response must therefore be just as forceful: We must send a clear message to all hatemongers that their bigotry will not be tolerated.

German leadership has been painfully slow in articulating its opposition to violence. Hopefully, our Supreme Court will not make the same mistake by declaring state legislation to protect hate-crime victims unconstitutional. Indeed, if we do not quickly mobilize our forces in the interest of tolerance, the continuing wave of European violence could serve as a mirror image of our own future.

Are We Seeing a Backlash to Hate Crime Legislation?

Jack McDevitt and Jack Levin prepared this essay for the newsletter of the California Association of Human Relations Organization (Winter 1999). They express concern that hate crime laws will fall victim to a distortion and misunderstanding of their purpose.

The measure of a backlash is often reflected in efforts to reverse previous legislative decisions—for example, opponents of affirmative action mustered enough support, two years ago, to pass California's Proposition 209 and now press for passage of Washington State's pending Proposition 200.

Perhaps inspired by their anti-affirmative action brethren, the forces of resistance to hate crime laws are now also making their move into mainstream America. Judging by the quantity of newspaper and magazine editorials taking a minimalist point of view, it appears that we are about to do for hate crime legislation what we are in the process of doing for affirmative action—namely, to eliminate a much needed government policy for the sake of ideology.

The latest incarnation of the backlash has targeted efforts to pass a bill at the federal level that would offer assistance to local law enforcement in hate crimes motivated by sexual orientation, disability, or gender. Representative of this viewpoint, legal scholar Kimberly Potter has recently argued, for example, that federal legislation is unnecessary, redundant, even counterproductive.

Her argument is a half-truth: While it is true that 39 states already have some kind of anti-hate crime statute, such state laws usually do not offer the protection offered by the proposed federal legislation. Most states protect victims who are targeted because of their race, religion, and ethnicity, but only 19 include victimization by sexual orientation and another 20 cover victimization by disability.

Affirmative action is perceived, rightly or wrongly, as giving special treatment to certain groups at the expense of other groups. Riding on the coattails of this popular argument, those who would abolish hate crime laws say the same thing. They claim that hate crime statutes are divisive because they protect only "special groups" such as blacks or gays. Nothing could be farther from the truth. In fact, according to every state hate crime statute as well as the proposed federal version, each and every American potentially receives protection. Such statutes criminalize acts that are motivated by the fact that victims are different from the perpetrator. Thus, straights are as likely to be protected as gays and lesbians. Whites who are attacked are as likely as blacks or Asians or Latinos to be protected by the law. Of all the racially motivated incidents reported to the FBI in 1996 (the most recent data available), some 20 percent involved white victims. In Todd Mitchell vs. The State of Wisconsin, the U.S. Supreme Court upheld the constitutionality of hate crime statutes in a case involving an attack on a white victim by a group of African-American teenagers.

Critics of hate crime laws argue also that by passing legislation at the national level, the Federal Government will take jurisdiction away from local authorities in hate crime cases. While it is unlikely that the FBI will add significantly to its staff in this area, there is indeed a legitimate concern about the most appropriate use of limited federal resources.

At last week's meeting of the International Association of Chiefs of Police in Salt Lake City, Attorney General Janet Reno discussed her belief that the Federal government should have a limited role in hate crime prosecutions. According to the Attorney General, the FBI will continue to offer technical assistance and investigative support to local law enforcement but does not intend, in many cases, to initiate federal prosecutions. Reno's intention is backed by history: the Justice Department has prosecuted fewer than 40 hate crime cases between 1992 and 1997 (during this period the FBI documented more than 20,000 local hate crime cases). In the recent tragedy in Jasper Texas, for example, where a black man was dragged to his death behind a pick-up truck, the federal government offered only support to local law enforcement. All prosecutions in the case have been handled locally.

The deterrent effect of hate crime statutes may be stronger than the opposition will admit. In some areas, legislation does in fact have a limited ability to deter, because the offender is willing to risk punishment to engage in criminal acts. This may be true in some drug crimes, for example. By contrast, hate crime offenders get very little in the way of material reward from their crimes, often no more than bragging rights with their friends. Therefore, increasing the risk of prosecution and incarceration might make such hate-motivated offenses far less appealing.

Hate crime legislation can serve as a deterrent in another way as well. Most hate offenses are committed by a group of perpetrators who are not unlike the four students involved in the gay-bashing and murder of Matthew Shepard in Laramie, Wyoming. Typically, there is one leader and a number of other young people who go along with their friends, because they don't know how to get themselves out of a bad situation. Having a strong hate crime law that is actively prosecuted may not dissuade a hardened hatemonger, but it may give the less committed participants in a bias crime enough reason to convince his buddies that the assault on a vulnerable victim is simply not worth the risk.

But even if it is true, as Potter and others have suggested, that hate crime laws—whether in Wyoming or at the federal level—would probably not have prevented the recent torture and murder of Matthew Shepard, there is every reason to support legislation. Most hate crimes are not murders—they are intimidations and threats that often escalate into much worse—unless they are stopped in their tracks. And that is precisely the point of hate crime legislation—it is designed to send a zero-tolerance message to both perpetrators and victims. To the perpetrators, such laws say loud and clear that Americans reject hatemongering in all of its forms and that they will no longer tolerate intolerance. To victims, hate crime laws suggest that law enforcement authorities will aggressively attempt to apprehend the offenders, even if it means bringing in the FBI.

Laws play many roles in our society. It is true that legislation allows us to prosecute those who commit acts against society, but legislation also reflects the values that the members of a society hold. We use some laws as symbolic statements of our values. For example, many states have laws requiring that adults stand during the playing of our national anthem. Such statutes are seldom enforced but they reflect the importance that we place on patriotism. Similarly, hate crime legislation reflects our collective belief that we Americans are stronger when all of our people have an equal opportunity to participate in democracy.

Perhaps for the first time in history, Americans have taken an initiative in reducing bigotry and prejudice, not because we are in the midst of a crisis, but simply because it is the right thing to do, because it will protect vulnerable people from harm. It would be a shame to abandon this basic American principle.

Shooting at the Ivory Tower

In this collaboration, which appeared in the Boston Globe *(September 9, 1990), we focus on hate-motivated violence against college students and tactics that universities have used to become better neighbors.*

It may be comforting to believe that the murders of five college students in Gainesville, Fla., were an isolated case. Unfortunately, they are part of a larger pattern of violence against college students.

Last year 14 female students at the University of Montreal were killed; three students at Brooklyn College were savagely beaten by a gang of teenagers; and teen-age gangs in Providence assaulted 27 Brown University students as part of an initiation ritual.

Violence against college students is, of course, nothing new. Charles Whitman gunned down 14 students at the University of Texas in 1966; serial killers Ted Bundy and John Norman Collins chose the college campus as the target for their killing sprees. Yet, the current wave of campus violence is different: It is perpetrated not by fellow students on the basis of convenience, but by an outsider who selects his victims precisely because they are college students.

Education has long been regarded as the pathway to success in America. But federal cutbacks in student loans and skyrocketing tuition costs have effectively placed a college education beyond the reach of many Americans. Perhaps for minorities more than for other Americans, higher education has become a symbol of disenfranchisement rather than hope.

Only 28 percent of all college-aged black Americans attended college in 1988, down from 33 percent in 1976. Hispanic enrollment during the same period dropped from 36 percent to 31 percent. As a result, growing numbers of minority and disadvantaged Americans feel excluded.

The National Task Force for Minority Achievement in Higher Education has warned that a failure to make sure that college populations reflect the nation's cultural diversity "will create a permanent second class citizenry."

The universities must help reverse this trend. They must change their image and orientation from that of exclusivity to access. Many private institutions have traditionally maintained scholarship programs for students who are in financial need. These programs, however, fail to address the problems and needs of the communities in which these schools are located.

Fortunately, some colleges and universities are taking steps to recruit larger numbers of disadvantaged students from surrounding inner-city neighborhoods. Their approach is based upon the philanthropic work of Eugene Lang who in 1981 "adopted" a graduating class of sixth graders in East Harlem and assisted them financially through college.

In the "Say Yes to Education" program in Philadelphia, 112 sixth graders have been promised full college support by the University of Pennsylvania if they finish high school. Similarly, Northeastern University recently announced a scholarship program targeted at 100 Boston public school first graders who will be granted full scholarships upon receiving a high school diploma.

Such programs would not only reduce the level of campus violence but also provide access to Americans desperate for opportunity.

■ ■ ■ ■ ■

PART VI

SERIAL MURDER

■ ■ ■ ■ ■

Serial Killers: How the Statistics Mislead Us

We wrote this essay, published in the Boston Herald *(December 1, 1985), during the height of the 1980s serial murder panic. At that time, Americans had grown concerned that serial killers were lurking around every corner.*

The body counts—or rather guesses—surrounding the recently discovered murders in Calaveras County, California are as confusing as they are alarming. Some reports suggest at least 25 victims; others speculate near 40.

It is easy to be misled into thinking that these figures represent real bodies and hard evidence. To the contrary, investigators have found evidence of only nine bodies plus several bags full of bones. The figures are based on the number of missing persons who may have come into contact with the suspected killers, Leonard Lake and Charles Ng.

If history repeats itself, we can expect these estimates to err on the high side. A prime example is the case of convicted serial killer Henry Lee Lucas. Having previously claimed responsibility for as many as 360 slayings, Lucas now insists that he killed "only" one. The evidence suggests that the truth is somewhere in between. Lucas's detailed recollection of facts that only the killer could know implicates him in dozens of homicides.

On the other hand, the dates and locales of some of these murders would make his self-proclaimed 36-state killing spree logistically impossible. Should we be surprised that a man would wish to cast himself as America's most deadly killer and that the nation would swallow his story so uncritically?

Hardly. From Lucas' point of view, his motivations were self serving: So long as he confessed to new crimes, this illiterate and once-obscure drifter remained in the limelight and off death row. His eagerness to confess gave police investigators around the country the potential opportunity to clear up unsolved homicides, no matter how tenuous the evidence

Altogether, these occasional arrests of serial killers serve to alarm and satisfy our society, which has been led to believe (by no less an authority than the Justice Department) that at least 35 such killers are on the loose in the United States, taking thousands of lives every year.

To support its contention, the Justice Department cites the rise to 25 percent of homicides those with "unknown motive." But this does not mean that all or even a majority of these 5,000 homicides are committed with "no apparent motive."

The distinction between "no motive" and "unknown motive" is easily lost. For example, the August 1984 *Life* magazine article on serial murder began with the absurd but frightening headline, "Serial Murderers Kill 5,000 of Us Every Year." Although inaccurate, such statistics serve well the interests of those who want us to believe that there is a serial murder epidemic.

Just how many of these 5,000 homicides with unknown motives could be the work of serial killers? When pressed, law enforcement experts told *Newsweek* that "as many as two-thirds of the estimated 5,000 unsolved homicides in the nation each year may be committed by serial murderers." Even this estimate is, to say the least, far-fetched.

If, as suggested by the Justice Department, there were 35 serial killers on the loose—people taking lives at random for the sake of pleasure or sexual gratification—they would have to average 100 victims per killer per year to meet the authorities' farfetched claim. Even Henry Lee Lucas, in his wildest fantasies, didn't purport to achieve this rate of killing. His alleged total of 360 victims took him eight years to compile.

We found in a survey that we conducted of multiple murders—both massacres and serial killings of at least four victims—that they are indeed on the rise. In the last two decades, the number of mass slayings has grown to the point that they now account for several hundred victims per year, far fewer than the thousands estimated by the "experts."

Our data show that, at present, there are 50 known mass murders each year, only 20 percent of which are serial killings. The additional number of serial killers who remain at large and undetected could hardly propel the annual victim count into the thousands.

The menace of mass murder is not to be found just in its numbers, but more in the excessive fear that has been encouraged by exaggerated statements concerning the scope and character of this crime.

The Justice Department has "discovered" the new genre of "serial killer," by definition someone who "roams the country," sometimes traveling hundreds of thousands of miles to kill at random. This image implies that no one is safe. After all, he may be in your town next!

Again, our data are at odds with what the Justice Department suggests. We found that the majority of serial killers do not travel widely; they take their victims from their own communities while leading otherwise normal lives. More typical than nomadic killers Ted Bundy and Christopher Wilder are those who killed In one area. These include Angelo Buono, Albert De-Salvo, John Wayne Gacy, David Berkowitz, Wayne Williams and Dean Corll.

Just as we attempted to understand the motivations for overstating the volume and scope of Lucas' murders, we have to ask why blatantly inaccurate statements concerning the size and scope of the "serial-murder problem" have been publicized without challenge. From the standpoint of the Justice Department, this served well its attempts to secure funding for the VICAP (Violent Criminal Apprehension Program) initiative—a national computer system for tracking serial murderers.

More interesting and subtle is our tendency to view the world in absolutes: Unless it's big, it's not a problem. Statistics on missing children, drunken driving, domestic violence, drug abuse and serial murder may have been inflated to mobilize our nation in a drive to combat them.

The effectiveness notwithstanding, these exaggerated claims may have an unintended side effect—to breed a general sense of cynicism and distrust that ultimately affects all of our human relationships. Excessive fear that our children are imperilled as they walk home from school, that the driver in the next lane is so smashed that he can't see where he's going, that every bruise on a child implicates an abusive parent, that our public schools are high-volume markets in illicit drugs, and that the boy next door is a potential serial killer—all these anxieties may turn us into a nation of "pre-victims," paralyzed by suspicion and turned inward.

The Menace of Serial Murder

James Alan Fox prepared this essay for the Palm Beach Post
*(January 29, 1989). This profile explains the characteristics
and motivation of the serial murderer.*

It would be comforting if real-life serial killers looked and acted like those in
the movies. If they were glassy-eyed lunatics like Jason of *Friday the 13th,* we
would beware whenever they approached. If they were introverted loners
like *Psycho*'s Norman Bates, they could not charm us so easily into their deadly
clutches. The frightening truth is that serial killers, like Ted Bundy and John
Wayne Gacy, are extraordinarily ordinary and, therefore, so very dangerous.

There is a profile of the typical serial murderer. He is a white male in his
late twenties or thirties, who kills not for love, money, or revenge, but just for
the fun of it. Unlike most other types of murderers, the serial killer hardly
ever uses a firearm. A gun would only rob him of his greatest pleasure: exult-
ing in his victim's suffering. The serial killer satisfies his hunger for power and
control by squeezing from his victim's body its last breath of life.

Most people would assume that anyone who kills for fun must be crazy.
Some serial killers have been driven by insanity, such as Herbert Mullen of
Santa Cruz, California who killed 13 people in a span of four months in order
to avert an earthquake. Most, however, are not insane in either a legal or
medical sense. Serial killers know right from wrong, know exactly what they
are doing, can control their desire to kill, but choose not to do so.

Psychologically, the serial killer is a sociopath, which is a disorder of
character rather than of the mind. He lacks a conscience, feels no remorse,
and cares exclusively for his own pleasures in life. Other people are seen
merely as tools to fulfil his own needs and desires, no matter how perverse
or reprehensible.

Researchers are not of one mind in explaining what causes sociopathy.
Some emphasize genetic factors, while others point to early childhood de-
fects, such as insufficient bonding of the child to his parents or even physical
and psychological abuse. Indeed, the biographies of most serial killers reveal
significant psychological trauma at an early age, but then so do the biographies of many successful people as well.

Whenever the case of an infamous serial killer is examined, we invariably search for clues in the childhood that might explain his seemingly senseless murders. Many writers have emphasized Ted Bundy's concerns over being illegitimate, and biographers of Kenneth Bianchi, the so-called "Hillside Strangler" of Los Angeles, capitalized on his having been adopted. Had Mr. Bundy and Mr. Bianchi grown up to be ruthless business tycoons— unkind but successful—rather than infamous killers, their biographers would have pointed to the same childhood issues as hurdles, the overcoming of which had made them stronger individuals.

It has been estimated that one in twenty males in our society could be considered sociopathic. Of course, most sociopaths are not violent: they may lie, cheat, or steal, but rape and murder are not particularly appealing to them. The other critical ingredient to the profile of the serial killer is a strong tendency toward sexual sadism. If given to perverse sexual fantasy, the sociopath simply feels uninhibited by societal rules or by conscience from literally chasing his dreams.

The cause of sexual sadism is as elusive as that of sociopathy. Could Ted Bundy have been right in his eleventh-hour claim that pornography inspired him to kill, or was he just making excuses to deflect blame? It should be no surprise to anyone that the vast majority of serial killers do have keen interest in pornography, particularly sadistic magazines and films. Sadism is the source of their greatest pleasure, and so, of course, they experience it vicariously in their spare time, when not on the prowl themselves. That is, a preoccupation with pornography is a reflection of their own sexual desires, not the cause of them.

Even if we do not fully understand the root causes of sexual sadism or of sociopathy, could we not at least use these profile characteristics as early warning signs of a dangerous individual? Assuming that we were able legitimately to screen for these characteristics, we would confront the fact that thousands of men fit the profile of a serial killer and do not commit violent crimes, much less serial murder. In our democratic society, we cannot round up all the would-be serial killers just because they fit a profile. Unfortunately, we cannot prevent this crime because we cannot predict it in any reliably way.

It may seem so hopeless and frightening to think that serial killers look perfectly normal and, although having abnormal personality characteristics, cannot be identified in advance. It may ease our fears, however, to remember that serial murder is still a rare phenomenon.

Despite recent publicity concerning the modern serial murderer, there are at most 150 Americans killed each year by serial killers. In fact, the chance of falling victim to a serial murderer is less than that of contracting malaria.

Serial murder is a growing menace to be sure, but far from an epidemic. The most menacing aspect of the modern serial killer may be our fear of him. If we perceive every stranger we encounter as a potential serial killer, then we will be victimized in a much more insidious way by a sense of cynicism and distrust for our fellow human beings.

Andrew Cunanan: America's Bogey Man

In this essay prepared for the San Diego Union-Tribune *(July 25, 1997), we explain why a serial killer, raised in the San Diego area, became a focus of national attention...and fear.*

This week marks the sixth anniversary of the discovery of Jeffrey Dahmer's grisly slaughterhouse in Milwaukee. While the horror of Dahmer's crimes may have been unprecedented, he received considerably less media attention than the murders allegedly committed by Andrew Cunanan. Part of the reason, of course, is that the latest victim was celebrity Gianni Versace, rather than some marginalized person—for example, a prostitute, a homeless person, or a minority. Middle-class Americans seem to be vastly more concerned when the victim reminds them of themselves or even of their heroes.

Another reason for the pervasive interest is that we knew so much about the suspect. Though he avoided apprehension for months, Cunanan's identity was discovered shortly after the initial murders, permitting reporters everywhere to delve into every detail of his past for clues as to why he may have slain five people. Scores of his friends, acquaintances, colleagues, roommates, and family members were sought out for their insights and recollections by journalists and on-air interviewers. All of this, of course, made for good copy and good TV.

But the most important reason for the media saturation regarding Cunanan is the fact that he was totally unpredictable—he had been on the loose for months, was believed to have killed a broad range of people, and had roamed from state to state. When Jeffrey Dahmer captured the attention of Americans in 1991, he himself had already been captured. Americans were curious, repulsed, and even fascinated, but they weren't terrified.

Cunanan is another matter entirely: people were fascinated with him, but mainly so they could avoid being his next victim. After all, if he could show up in Minnesota, Illinois, New Jersey, and Florida, then he might have been in *your state, maybe even in your neighborhood or your house.*

Unfortunately, Cunanan's alleged killing spree fed into Americans' inordinate fear of crime, ironically at the very time that the crime rate is headed downward. Americans, however, do not develop a sense of insecurity from crime statistics; it is the rare but sensational event—a grisly murder on the front-page and the eleven o'clock news—that determines most people's perception of their own vulnerability.

For months, there were reports from Key West to San Francisco of Andrew Cunanan look-alikes. Part of the reason he was seen everywhere is that he looked like 20 million other people—extraordinarily ordinary— perhaps this is why he avoided apprehension for so long. A more important reason for the Cunanan sightings, however, involves excessive fear— eyewitness observation is notoriously unreliable, especially when the witnesses are scared to death. It is well known that rumors spread under conditions of anxiety—when people fear for their lives. Andrew Cunanan has become the modern version of the "bogey man."

Can the media really be blamed for giving so much attention to Andrew Cunanan? As long as a suspect is on the run, the press has not only a right but a responsibility to inform the public. Because the killer's primary victims seemed to be gay men, the gay community was at particular risk. Yet, at the same time, the killer had taken the lives of people who were simply in the wrong place at the wrong time. It is doubtful that Cunanan asked the New Jersey cemetery worker about his sexual orientation before he allegedly shot him and stole his pickup truck.

The latest string of serial killings reminds us that everyone is at risk, whether gay or straight, when a killer is on the loose. The degree of risk remains in question, however. Any given American is more likely to be killed by leprosy or malaria than by a serial killer. Any given motorist is more likely to be killed by a collision with a deer than by an encounter with someone like Andrew Cunanan. In the midst of intense media coverage, It is vitally important to keep in perspective the relationship between fear and murder. The risk of being victimized by a serial killer is rather small, but the risk of widespread paranoia could easily become epidemic.

Facts, Not Fluff

In this essay, written as a foreword to the book Technophobe: The
Unabomber Years, *we attempt to explain one of this country's most
enigmatic and elusive serial killers.*

The arrest of Theodore Kaczynski will hopefully bring to a close one of the
more extraordinary cases in the annals of crime. There are many ways in
which the Unabomber case broke the serial killer mold. Although most
serial murderers are cunning and clever, few have been so challenging for
law enforcement authorities by remaining at large and relatively active for
18 years. Few could hold an entire country—rather than some local community—in their grip of terror. And none has bargained so brazenly as in
the Unabomber's insistence that his so-called manifesto be published by
some of the nation's most prominent newspapers.

Notwithstanding these important differences, the Unabomber's motivation articulated in the manifesto is actually an inventive twist on a very
old theme among serial killers. Many of them have sought psychologically
to distance themselves from their crimes—to deny responsibility for their
horrendous misdeeds through excuse, justification or even alibi. While a
death-row inmate, for example, John Wayne Gacy penned an extensive if
undistinguished autobiography in which he proclaimed his innocence in the
brutal torture-murder of 33 men and boys. Some serial killers have exter-
nalized blame by implicating forces outside of themselves. The most famous
of such cases is Theodore Bundy who, just hours before being executed by
the State of Florida, confessed his hideous murders and then blamed them
on his exposure to violent pornography as a child. Still other serial murderers have sought to justify their slayings by claiming to have been on a mis-
sion of some sort—to have committed mercy killings, to have intended to
rid the world of evil, to have cleaned the streets of human trash, or to have
been directed by the voices of demons. That's why they murdered prostitutes, nursing home patients, or homeless people—or so they claim.

The Unabomber's manifesto was impressive not only for its post-modern,
anti-technology rationalization, but also for its 35,000 word length. Unlike
most other serial killers, the Unabomber had both the requisite intelligence

and education to craft an elaborate and extensive justification and then to demand that it be printed in papers no less prestigious than the *Washington Post* or *The New York Times.*

Capitulating to the Unabomber's literal version of "publish or perish," the *Washington Post* did finally print the manifesto word-for-word and in its entirety. From the point of view of the killer, the publication only confirmed his delusions of grandeur. Was he not special after all? Was he not the only person ever to have published such a lengthy piece in such a prestigious newspaper? In his own misguided mind, furthermore, it transformed him into some kind of folk hero—a high-tech Robin Hood, a humanitarian who had unselfishly dedicated his humble life to saving us from ourselves. He would be our savior by freeing us all from technological enslavement.

From the viewpoint of the *Post,* as well as the FBI, however, printing the manifesto ostensibly had a different purpose. It provided the American people with a set of clues that could be identified with the Unabomber's background and ultimately lead to his apprehension. If justifiable from a public-safety perspective, would this not have argued for publication in the *Sunday New York Times,* which, unlike the daily *Post,* would have been widely available everywhere, especially in the vicinities of Chicago and San Francisco? The somewhat contradictory decision was made, however, to print in the daily *Post* in order to satisfy the killer's demands in the least obtrusive way.

In the end, of course, David Kaczynski did in fact recognize strong similarities between portions of the Unabomber's manifesto and his own brother's writings—certain idiosyncracies in syntax and substance that were too obvious to ignore. But this recognition came months after excerpts from the manifesto were disseminated widely and months *before* the controversial *Washington Post* edition.

Whether or not the manifesto's publication was a critical element to the discovery of the Unabomber's identity, its anti-technology message clearly appeals to numerous Americans who feel as though they have been victimized by robotics, automation, and computers. By focusing so closely on the Unabomber's manifesto, however, we may have obscured an important aspect of his motivation for killing. As a young man, the Unabomber found support for his Luddite philosophy in the counterculture of the hip generation, which was highly critical of modern society and stressed an alternative lifestyle. At this point, he probably also fit the profile of the typical workplace avenger—a man who goes on a rampage at the office after being fired or laid off. Indeed, he may have had a particular grievance against a company, a university, or an industry in which he had held a position.

As he matured into middle-age, however, the Unabomber's motivation may have changed. Rather than being inspired by social philosophy, he perhaps enjoyed killing for its own sake. Not unlike a sadistic serial killer who is obsessed with power, control, and dominance, the Unabomber enjoyed the thrill of terrorizing an entire nation, felt superior playing a game of cat and mouse with the FBI (which he regarded as incompetent), and gained a sense of mastery by building bombs that would injure his victims from a distance of thousands of miles. He spent day after day, isolated from the society that he despised, sitting in the local library in order to read about himself in newspapers around the country.

If the Unabomber is a power-hungry serial killer, why did he murder from a distance? Most serial killers love the physical contact with their victims. They are typically sexual sadists who would never distance themselves from the people they torture and kill. That is why so few serial killers use a firearm, why they almost always kill with their hands.

The intense brutality of their crimes is made possible, for most serial killers, by the fact that they are sociopaths—men who are incapable of feeling warmth or empathy. They kill with moral impunity. Unlike most other serial killers, however, the Unabomber may have had a conscience and so he could not face his victims. In his own thinking, he destroyed merely demonized abstractions—dehumanizing institutions, uncaring industries, dangerous companies—rather than flesh-and-blood human beings. Thus, the Unabomber's manifesto was important not only in its ability to justify his killing spree to the members of society, but also to rationalize his hideous crimes to himself. And because of his reclusive, isolated lifestyle, no one was around to dispel his increasingly fanatical world view.

One of the most curious aspects of the Unabomber case has been the public reaction following the capture of Theodore Kaczynski. Despite the despicable nature of the murders and maimings that he is alleged to have committed, Kaczynski has been treated with an odd and unjustified degree of sympathy. Now that the Unabomber threat is presumably over, there is more an atmosphere of fun and festivity than indignant condemnation. Not only have Unabomber t-shirts hit the streets, but Americans have laughed along with Jay Leno's nightly monologue and skits about the Montana hermit. Some Americans have gone so far as to organize Unabomber fan clubs and legal defense funds.

Whether guilty or not, Theodore Kaczynski clearly does not deserve the glamorized attention that he has received since his arrest. If guilty, he is a cold-blooded killer, not a hero. For this reason, for example, we prefer to call him "Theodore," as his mother may have done years ago when she was annoyed with him, rather than the more familiar nickname "Ted" used for someone who is a good friend.

It is our desire to shed light on the Unabomber, but definitely not a spotlight. To understand his crimes fully, we need facts, not fluff. By examining this case in detail and with a dispassionately analytical eye, we can learn much about a variety of trends ongoing in America. By studying the extreme, we can learn about what motivates more commonplace instances of violent behavior as well as about the growing mood of resentment in this country.

PART VII

CULTURE OF KILLING

We're Veering off Course

Published in the Boston Herald *(January 18, 1998), this column was inspired by a Hamilton, Massachusetts family that refused to pay taxes despite a confrontation at their home with federal agents. Jack Levin explains how this unusual case reflects a more usual theme at the national level.*

What does the estate standoff in Hamilton have in common with the mass suicide of 39 Heaven's Gate cultists near San Diego and the Oklahoma City massacre?

The Sweeneys' failure to vacate their hillside residence provides another example of Americans who are turning, in ever increasing numbers, to the margins of society—rather than to its mainstream—for solutions to their personal problems.

Twenty or 30 years ago, citizens searching for spiritual guidance would, in all likelihood, have received comfort and reassurance from their church and family.

Those seeking a political answer would have found it in the Democratic or Republican parties. Now they are more likely to join an obscure cult, go into the woods on Sunday afternoons to rehearse for the coming apocalypse, or simply barricade themselves in their home rather than obey a federal court order.

All of our traditional institutions are under attack. Post-modernists turn their backs on the scientific method, claiming that it has helped to destroy civilization; skeptical patients experiment with herbal or homeopathic medicine, mega-vitamin therapy, acupuncture, or tai chi; and increasing numbers of parents have given up on public schools, opting for a private-school alternative or for educating their youngsters at home.

Their credibility with the American people having plummeted to new depths, our leaders now have the stature of stereotypical used-car salesmen.

In a recent Gallup survey, only nine percent of adult Americans voiced a great deal of confidence in the executive branch of government, only 10 percent in Congress.

Three-quarters of Americans are convinced the government is somehow involved in conspiracies, and two in five Americans continue to believe it has covered up information about the TWA 800 jet disaster. Pierre Salinger is far from the Lone Ranger when it comes to being suspicious of the FBI or the CIA.

Outside of government, moreover, our institutions are faring only slightly better. When asked to evaluate the honesty and ethical standards of various occupational groups, less than 20 percent of the American people gave very high marks to labor union leaders, real estate agents, lawyers, stockbrokers, business executives, newspaper reporters, TV commentators, bankers, police, dentists, medical doctors, college teachers, or even clergy.

Part of the reason for the erosion of trust and confidence in traditional institutions involves the eclipse of community we have recently experienced. Many Americans feel they have no place to turn when they get into trouble—they are unable to find a sense of belonging or importance at work, among friends, or in their own families.

Children come home from school to an empty house. Anxious not to be fired or laid off, their parents are too busy at work to get to know their neighbors or participate in community activities.

Those who have moved their residence for the sake of a job no longer have friends, family, or fraternal organizations to help them through tough times. Their support systems are now hundreds, perhaps thousands, of miles away.

Even if they have remained in the same community, growing numbers of families are without the assistance of extended kin, especially grandparents; growing numbers of children lack two parents who can share the tasks of child-rearing and bread-winning.

As income inequality continues to rise, the eclipse of community becomes increasingly burdensome. The decline in institutional credibility also involves a 30-year spiral of scandals involving leadership at the highest levels of government, business, and entertainment—Chappaquiddick, Abscam, Watergate, Irangate, the S&L bailout, Travelgate, Filegate, Whitewater and the recent campaign financing fiasco—not to mention the assumed and actual transgressions committed by Robert Packwood, Newt Gingrich, Bill Clinton, Michael Milken, Leona Helmsley, and Michael Jackson, among many others.

As we approach the year 2000, growing numbers of Americans are thinking in apocalyptic terms. Some expect a spiritual transition to a higher plane, while others believe the new millennium will bring the ultimate physical confrontation and destruction in a war of all against all.

We cannot do anything to alter the calendar—we can only hope our nation will survive and reach new heights in the next millennium. As individuals, we are almost as powerless to influence the course of our economy at the federal level.

But all of us can assume a special sense of responsibility for what happens in our own back yard—at work, in our neighborhoods and schools, and at home. It is at the grass-roots level that we might begin to repair the credibility of our traditional institutions. This is where we can make an effort on behalf of our fellow citizens in trouble, so that they feel important, special, a sense of belonging, like they really count.

Bringing Americans back into the mainstream may be our only realistic chance to prevent more mass suicides, acts of domestic terrorism and citizen standoffs in the future.

A Culture That's Ripe
to Sustain Evil

In this essay prepared for the Boston Herald *(May 11, 1999), we explain and critique aspects of popular culture in which "evil deeds" and "evil doers" are shamelessly celebrated.*

In an attempt to explain the recent school massacres in Jonesboro, West Paducah, Pearl, and Littleton, many commentators have implicated the prevalence of violence in television, films, and video games. Not only has the First Lady made this her latest soap box issue, but the White House has planned a summit focusing on the effects of entertainment on youth violence. Right or wrong, they still may have missed a far more important point: Americans have created a popular culture in which evil is celebrated.

The most popular of the morality plays of yesteryear have gone the way of *Leave It To Beaver*—and with them America's heroes. Only the bad guys remain to serve as role models for our children. Everywhere you look in our popular culture, you find villainy.

Professional wrestling provides an apt metaphor for viewing such changes in America. Until recently, the typical wrestling match consisted of the powerful and virtuous good guys (dressed in white tights adorned with stars and stripes) who almost always beat the physically and morally inferior bad guys (dressed in menacing black costumes). But professional wrestling of the 1990s has instead become dominated by darkness and brutality—opponents are set on fire, hit with a barbed wire baseball bat, or dumped into a garbage bin and carried away on a stretcher. The traditional good guy has been written out of the script.

Talk shows of the 1980s—Oprah, Donahue, and the like—similarly featured good against evil—the abusive or womanizing husband versus his victimized wife; the child who terrorized his classmates. Audience members would typically boo and hiss the villain and support the victims. But Jerry Springer's youthful audience now cheers wildly as equally sleazy guests pound one another with their fists as the cameras role. And Springer is now more popular than Oprah—especially with eighth graders.

Prime-time TV programs have traditionally included a variety of contests—westerns and police dramas—in which the guys with the white hats ultimately defeated the forces of evil. Today, such dramatic series on TV are more likely to focus on the complexities of morality, rather than its virtues. Chuck Norris's *Walker, Texas Ranger* is one of the few programs to retain a morality play aspect, and it is routinely attacked by critics who regard it as the most violent program on television. They, too, have missed the point.

We used to put our heroes on pedestals where they could be admired, revered, and emulated, but those days are long gone. Today's children grow up collecting trading cards which bear the images of mass murderers rather than baseball players. On their bedroom walls, youngsters hang calenders featuring Ted Bundy and the Hillside Strangler. Instead of chronicling the good deeds of superheroes, cartoons and comics today depict the seedier side of life. Batman and Robin have been supplanted by Beavis and Butthead as well as South Park, the conquests of Superman have been replaced by a comic-book version of Jeffrey Dahmer. Children can also locate killer web sites, wear killer t-shirts, and join killer fan clubs. They listen to the lyrics of Marilyn Manson who inspires them to try Satanism, vampirism, Gothic fashion, and mass murder.

Why have we abandoned hero worship? The answer is clear: Our traditional exemplars have let us down; our idols have feet of clay. Over the last 30 years, there have been repeated scandals at the highest levels of government, industry, and entertainment—Chappaquiddick, Watergate, Abscam, Irangate, Whitewater, Filegate, S&L, Monicagate, and campaign financing violations. Even worse, former heroes have been accused of engaging in major acts of crime and corruption—for example, Hulk Hogan (steroids), Pete Rose (illegal gambling), Mark McGwire (a diet supplement), Mike Tyson (rape), Hugh Grant (cavorting with a prostitute), Michael Jackson (child molestation), Pee Wee Herman (indecent exposure), Chris Farley (drug abuse), Michael Milken (insider trading), Bob Packwood (sexual harassment), O. J. Simpson (murder), and Bill Clinton (womanizing and sexual assault).

The latest Americans celebrated for their evil ways are the two Littleton teenaged shooters. While most youngsters around America have rightly identified with the victims' pain and suffering, too many children instead identify with the power of the perpetrators. What is more, Harris and Klebold became instant celebrities when they had their photos plastered across the covers of magazines and newspapers, coast to coast, inspiring a series of copycats seeking their own fifteen minutes of infamy.

Celebrating evil has turned morality inside out, making heroes into villains and villains into heroes. We no longer trust our traditional role models, because they have too often let us down. Notorious criminals, on the other hand, may not have the virtues we would like our children to emulate, but at least they will never disappoint us.

Two Thumbs Down
for TV Ratings

In this piece written for the Boston Sunday Herald *(October 18, 1998), we take to task recently launched measures for restricting children's access to violent television programming.*

Recent research from the Henry J. Kaiser Family Foundation suggests that the television networks are failing to assign appropriate ratings for all of their shows, denying parents the opportunity to supervise their children's entertainment choices. Kathryn Montgomery, president of the Center for Media Education, lamented that the much heralded and long-awaited V-Chip will fail unless the ratings system can be fine-tuned. To the contrary, we say, "bravo," "excellent," "wonderful," and "terrific." Keep the V-Chip away from parents; eliminate TV ratings so that mommy and daddy will not be tempted to rely on them.

The V-Chip is, of course, a simple technological device to permit parents to control their kids' viewing habits. Through a computer chip to be installed in all new TVs sold as of 2000, parents will be able to pre-program their sets to screen out shows that have been rated as violent (or that have sexual content). Thanks to the V-Chip, they can have remote-control over their children's viewing selections, all the way from the office.

The heart of the problem lies in the rating concept itself. There has been much debate in recent years about what kind of ratings we should have flash on the corner of the TV screen. Should we use content ratings, such as V for violence, N for nudity, L for language, and FV for fantasy violence? Or, should TV follow the example of the movies, and use age-based ratings, such as TV-G, TV-PG, and TV-M? In our way of thinking, neither approach makes any sense. Indeed, the best ratings are no ratings at all.

To see the problem with ratings, consider what happened to films some two decades ago, when the voluntary motion picture code went into effect. The movies actually got more violent, not less. Film makers began to add gratuitous violence, sex, nudity or language in order to achieve a higher—or better—rating. An R rating was, of course, most desirable for ticket sales, and a G-rating was virtually the kiss of death at the box office. So, motion pictures became increasingly filled with graphic scenes of unimaginable gore and sex to boost box office appeal.

Experimental studies have clearly shown that movie-goers—particularly teenagers—are most attracted to the media version of "forbidden fruit"—to films that carry an R rating or a parental warning. Of course, if you're not part of the "mature audience," then that must make you part of the "immature audience," and what self-respecting kid wants to be labeled that?

Now, regrettably, we have ratings on television shows, thanks to a compromise solution to the media violence problem negotiated between Congress and the television industry. The rating code, however, is more a guide for children in determining what is a "must see" than a guide for parents on what their children must not see. Kids can now easily scan *TV Guide* to circle the programs labeled TV-MA or have a L, S, or V along side.

As a consequence of the rating system, TV script writers will be encouraged to do all they can to spice up programs in order to ensure a higher violence/sex/language rating. Without that, viewership and thus advertising revenues may be in jeopardy. So, throw in a little gratuitous sex or violence; fill the sound track with obscenities or suggestive humor; make the program appealing to the broadest possible age range.

The networks can guiltlessly infuse their programming with even more blood and guts, sex and provocative themes by appealing to the parental control over the V-Chip. "You parents," they can claim, "you've got the power, you've got the control. If you don't want your kids to watch *Friday the 13th–Part 72* or *Sex and the Single Senator,* then chip it out. It's *your* responsibility, not ours!"

The V-Chip will fail, but for reasons that Ms. Montgomery and other V-Chip supporters may not have considered. First of all, even though all new sets will have one, it will take years before all TV sets in every American home (including the old hand-me-down set in your child's bedroom attached to his Nintendo set) are equipped with the device; and don't count on the V-Chip box for older sets to be a big Christmas seller. And then how long will it take until parents forget how to program their V-Chips, if not lose the remote control altogether? These are the same folks whose VCRs constantly flash 12:00.

How long will it take until parents accede to the nagging demands of their kids to forget about the V-Chip? Or how long will it take until Johnnie finds a friend to visit whose parents don't really care about choosing their child's entertainment? Why stay home and watch *Bugs Bunny* when your new buddy is watching *Bugsy* on HBO?

Finally, the ratings and V-Chip technology will do nothing to control violent movie tapes on the VCR, video games which make killing scores of innocent people a cybersport, tabloid shows like *Hard Copy* (not to mention the news), or even tasteless squawk shows.

Parents, if they are relentless, may be able to V-Chip away sex and violence in the afternoon, but what viewing options will their children have? Even if parents effectively use their V-Chips, what will their kids do as an alternative? Watch Public Broadcasting? Read Shakespeare? If we want kids to tune out violence, we must give them something better to tune into. For the television industry, that may be the biggest challenge of all.

PART VIII

GUNS

The Gun Control Debate
Needs Some Middle Ground

As we completed this collection of essays, the issue of gun control once again took center stage in the national agenda. In response, Jack Levin suggests that the gun debate is more complex than either side appears willing to admit.

Is it really people, and not their guns, that kill? The problem with the gun control debate is that it is constantly being framed in all or nothing, absolute terms: guns vs. gun owners, the NRA vs. the Million Mom March, criminals vs. law-abiding citizens, the Second Amendment vs. government repression, and the like.

Does gun control actually reduce murder? The truth will satisfy almost nobody because it lies in the gray area between gun control zealots and gun fanatics: In reality, it all depends on what type of control measure is being advocated and on what kind of killing is being addressed.

Banning assault weapons: Most of the large-scale massacres have been committed with semi-automatics. Get rid of AK-47s and you would most likely reduce the massive body counts. The problem is that fewer than one percent of all murder victims—about 200 a year—lose their lives to a mass murderer. By contrast, some 19,000 annually are killed by a single bullet in a one-on-one confrontation. Eliminating high-power semiautomatics would do nothing to reduce single-victim murders and would have little impact on the overall rate of murder.

Enacting a waiting period and doing background checks: Most mass killers do not mind waiting. They have been known to do so for many months before opening fire at a crowded shopping mall, commuter train, or school. A waiting period of whatever length would therefore do almost nothing to reduce the possibility of a massacre at a school or a workplace. However, the Brady law's initial five-day waiting requirement was effective in providing a cooling off period for those enraged husbands, lovers, and friends who might spontaneously be angry enough to kill—if they had a loaded gun in their hands at the time.

Liberalizing concealed weapons laws: If almost everybody in town is packing heat, then you'd probably be safer doing the same. Certainly, a bank robber might think twice about pulling a loaded gun if he believes that all the customers and employees have one. Remember that the next time you visit Texas or Arkansas, where guns are as commonplace as chicken-fried steak. But just the opposite may be true in Massachusetts or Connecticut, where relatively few citizens carry firearms and the real problem is not murders committed by strangers, but by friends, family members, and neighbors who impulsively shoot one another. A liberal concealed weapons law might add to the murder rate by providing more of our citizens with a lethal means for resolving their everyday arguments, not only at home but also in bars, at restaurants, on the job, not to mention the roads in and out of town during commuting hours.

Enacting gun buyback programs: The Million Mom Marchers were in favor of this measure. Gun buyback programs have some symbolic importance, but do little more. People who turn in their guns can turn around and buy another, even more efficient model. And those individuals who plan to use their firearms in the near future are hardly the people who are likely to turn them in for cash.

Attaching gun locks: George W. Bush supports this measure. Anything that reduces the access of children to a loaded firearm might help. But it is doubtful that substantial numbers of gun-owners will use gunlocks, especially if they want immediate access to a weapon in order to defend themselves from intruders.

Educating children about the danger of firearms: The NRA is really pushing this approach, yet parental and classroom instructions typically do not generalize to the playground where youngsters are more persuaded by peers than by parents and teachers. A child who is bent on revenge, holds membership in a dangerous gang, or deals illicit drugs might actually rely on his firearm training to instruct him in the most effective manner of killing. On the other hand, educating children about the danger of guns might reduce at least some of the accidental shootings that result in death.

It is often said that if we make guns difficult to obtain, then only the criminals will be able to get them. This argument makes the dubious distinction between the good guys without guns and the bad guys who use them on the good guys. Actually, most lethal injuries are inflicted not by hardened gun-toting outlaws but by people who accidentally shoot one another, leave their guns in places accessible to their children who shoot one another, or lose their cool and impulsively shoot one another.

Almost every American recognizes we need to limit the availability of firearms. But rather than continue to debate a false and divisive issue, we should now focus on which gun control measures are effective and which ones are a waste of our time. There is much common ground in the gun control argument, but only if we get beyond the extremists on both sides.

Bush Blocks Fight Against Assault Guns

James Alan Fox published this column in the Palm Beach Post *(March 21, 1989) shortly after the attack on a California elementary school in which five children were shot to death. He criticizes then President George Bush for his weak response to the availability of assault weapons.*

Although it took the tragic deaths of five innocent children to inspire action, encouragingly a number of jurisdictions have moved to prohibit the sale of semiautomatic attack rifles like the one used by Patrick Purdy at a Stockton, Calif., schoolyard.

Whatever momentum has mounted toward making our society safer for all citizens is being eroded, however, by the reluctance of President George Bush to turn his back on the National Rifle Association.

Mr. Bush has argued that the states have adequate laws to punish criminals who commit crimes with guns and that the courts simply need to punish offenders to the fullest extent of the law. He believes that the solution lies in a tougher criminal justice system, rather than in restrictions on the availability of high-powered rifles.

Mr. Bush's position overlooks one significant point, however, at least in reference to tragedies such as the Stockton mass murder. Patrick Purdy is not alive for us to punish him. After killing five schoolchildren and wounding 28 other youngsters as well as two teachers, Purdy turned the gun on himself.

In fact, mass killers like Patrick Purdy, and like James Huberty who murdered 21 people, including many children, at a San Ysidro, Calif., Mc-Donald's in 1984, are frequently killed by their own hand or by police, before we ever get a chance to prosecute under those laws in which Mr. Bush places so much faith.

Even those mass killers who survive to be tried for their crimes are relatively unconcerned about the legal consequences. They care more about getting even, going as far as to slaughter society's most cherished members—its young children—than they do about their own lives.

I have heard the slogans of the gun enthusiasts: "Guns don't kill, people do." While NRA supporters are quite correct that guns are not to blame per se for the behavior of mass killers, guns, and attack rifles in particular, do make their crimes far bloodier.

It is nearly impossible to slay five children and wound 30 others with a knife or with one's hands. Regardless of the causes of the murderous impulses, the mass killer must have access to a means of mass destruction, and our nation certainly makes it easy enough for these embittered men to purchase all the guns and ammunition needed for a bloodbath.

In addition to the greater lethality of the firearm, guns distance the attacker psychologically from his victims. It is arguable that Patrick Purdy, for example, might not have been emotionally able to kill young children had he had any physical contact with his victims. But with a firearm, he could dispassionately shoot down anonymous children, as if they were moving objects in a video game or even soldiers on an imagined battlefield.

The Stockton tragedy convinced many fence-straddlers of the absurdity of our policies toward attack weapons. Responding to changing public mood, George Bush has also softened his position somewhat, but only with great hesitation.

The Bush administration, through "drug czar" William Bennett, has temporarily halted the importation of semiautomatic assault weapons. At the same time however, Mr. Bush has repeated his firm opposition to any interference with the domestic sale of this class of firearm.

Overall, the recent Bush concessions are token and wholly inadequate. It would not have mattered to the slain children of Stockton had the semiautomatic rifle used by Patrick Purdy been stamped "Made in USA." They would be just as dead.

During the campaign when debating the issue of abortion, Mr. Bush frequently boasted that he was "for life." I would presume that his deep regard for human life is not just limited to unborn fetuses. It may be too late for the five schoolchildren of Stockton, but not for the victims of future mass murderers who will take advantage of our permissive gun laws.

How many more innocent children must be slaughtered before Mr. Bush moves to disarm our society? Or, if he is truly a steadfast, card-carrying member of the NRA and cannot be swayed, can he live with their deaths?

The Assault Weapons Ban Does More Harm than Good

A version of this argument against laws banning semiautomatics was published in the Boston Globe *(May 15, 1996). In this piece, Jack Levin argues that laws banning assault weapons may actually backfire.*

Thanks to the prevalence of rapid-fire weaponry, some 200 Americans are killed every year by mass murderers carrying semiautomatics such as UZIs and AK-47s. In fact, eight of the 10 largest massacres in American history have occurred since 1980. Twenty-one innocent people were slain in San Ysidro, California; twenty-three in Killeen, Texas, fourteen in Edmond, Oklahoma, and so on. Among the most sizable mass killings, the April 1995 bombing of the federal building in Oklahoma City was a rare exception, because it did not depend on guns.

Considering these facts, the federal ban on so-called assault weapons sounds like a worthy piece of legislation—but for America's sake, I strongly oppose it.

One problem with the ban is that the majority of the 15,000 homicides by guns committed every year in this country are not multiple murders at all, but involve a single victim. To kill one person, perpetrators hardly need semiautomatic capability or a large capacity magazine. A small-caliber single-shot handgun is lethal enough.

Even worse, a continuing federal ban on assault weapons—not unlike pending legislation in New York State and Massachusetts—will make criminals out of marginal and alienated Americans who are already certain that the United States government, the United Nations, and the Federal Reserve Bank have ganged up against them.

The Freemen standoff outside of Jordan, Montana gives us a clue as to a frightening consequence of legislation to eliminate assault weapons by prosecuting gun owners. Members of militias, survivalists and so-called patriots groups are sincerely convinced that the Second Amendment gives Americans an absolute right to bear arms of their choice and that enemies of freedom have already taken over the federal government.

For such individuals, firearms symbolize liberty. They believe that any legislation to remove guns from their hands originates with the forces of evil. Their position goes something like this: We are loyal to our Founding Fathers and to the Constitution. We are ready to die in order to preserve the Republic.

Just as during the prohibition era of the 1920s, members of these groups will simply ignore any law that seeks to take their guns. Instead, they will continue to stockpile high-powered weapons and wait for law enforcement personnel to show up to arrest them.

Because of its association with Waco, Ruby Ridge, and the Oklahoma City massacre, April 19th has become "Independence Day" for resentful Americans who detest what they believe to be the illegitimate intrusion of the government into their lives. Any ban on assault weapons only confirms their worst suspicions and sets up more and more possibilities for violent confrontations between law enforcement agents and alienated citizens.

Given the government's lack of credibility with these angry Americans, effective gun control efforts must aim at manufacturing rather than consumption, supply rather than demand.

In retrospect, perhaps Americans should never have allowed hundreds of millions of guns to circulate among our citizens. But, now that we have, it may be too late to remove them, without also removing the consent of the governed. America's obsession with firearms may be the price we pay to live in a country with an abundance of personal freedom.

PART IX

JUSTICE SYSTEM RESPONSE TO MURDER

Safety's on the Line

We published this essay in the Boston Sunday Globe *(August 31, 1997) in the wake of two seemingly unrelated events—the shooting deaths of three police officers in New Hampshire and the brutalization of a Haitian immigrant by members of the New York City Police Department. We argue that both can be traced to the role that the police are increasingly expected to play in the "war against crime."*

Aggressive police enforcement, while cutting crime, can magnify dangers and even public mistrust. The slayings of three New Hampshire police officers in one week display the dangers that law enforcement personnel face daily, in small towns and big cities alike, in attempting to protect citizens from criminals.

State Troopers Leslie Lord and Scott Phillips were shot to death by an embittered 67-year-old man, when they stopped his car August 19 in Colebrook. An Epsom police officer Jeremy Charron was gunned down last Sunday during a routine traffic check, not long after he returned from the funeral of his fellow officers.

At the same time, recent charges of police brutality in New York City conjure up a decidedly contrasting image: that of a police presence that has run amok, of public servants who terrorize citizens, of sadistic officers who feel they are above the law. Two weeks ago, officers in Brooklyn allegedly dragged Abner Louima, a Haitian immigrant, into a 70th Precinct restroom and sodomized him with the handle of a toilet plunger.

Seemingly contradictory, both sides of the police stories—the vulnerability in New Hampshire and the brutality in Brooklyn—are nonetheless linked.

The most difficult and dangerous situations for police officers are created by policies that require aggressive crime-fighting strategies: investigating suspicious persons; arresting suspects in burglaries, robberies, and drug-related incidents; and responding to disturbance calls in bars and domestic disputes. The more police are asked to stop motorists, confront suspects, or make arrests, the greater the potential for someone being killed or for using excessive force.

Under such circumstances, both the police and the suspect see one another as the enemy, so that even a minor confrontation can easily be transformed into open warfare.

In Brooklyn, the police had initially singled out Louima for his alleged participation in a street scuffle outside a Flatbush nightclub. In New Hampshire, the killings sprang from a couple of routine stops for traffic violations. In this day and age, it seems, that is all it takes for blood to flow.

In New York City, "zero-tolerance" policing in response to spiraling crime has succeeded in enhancing the quality of everyday life and in bringing more law and order to the streets. It has also placed the police in more confrontational situations with residents, especially marginalized groups, thereby raising the likelihood of unprofessional conduct, if not illegal behavior.

According to *Newsweek* magazine, allegations of excessive force against the police in New York City neighborhoods rose 62 percent during the first two years of its zero-tolerance policy of cracking down on all crime. Thus, even though effective in fighting much lawlessness, the public pressure to reduce the crime rate may have convinced power-hungry officers that they have a mandate to clean the streets of criminals, no matter how irresponsibly, unethically, or illegally they behave.

Not only have proactive police practices produced more dangerous confrontations with citizens, but the overall "get tough" approach to crime control has placed police directly in the line of fire. Last year, for example, a New York officer was shot in the face when he attempted to question a suspect who turned out to be a paroled habitual criminal. A year earlier, two officers were shot in the same station house restroom where Louima said he was assaulted.

Criminals are becoming increasingly desperate, faced with heightened prospects of the death penalty, life sentences for "third strike" felonies as repeat offenders, and other stiff sanctions. As never before, criminals seem willing to shoot it out with police rather than to be taken alive.

More generally, the problems of police misconduct and overreaction in the face of danger are much larger than displayed in the actions of a few bad apples who slipped through the recruitment screening process. To a great extent, the culture of policing itself has fostered the level of hostility between cops and criminals. Authorities speak of a "war against crime" and a "war against drugs," and virtually every police innovation is couched in combat terms—Operation this-or-that.

What makes that para-militaristic style more problematic is that it is difficult for public protectors to tell the good guys from the bad guys. Unlike an actual declared war between nations, "enemy troops" in crime wars do not wear uniforms to set them apart from civilians. Bad guys include not just murderers, drug dealers, car thieves, prostitutes, and pimps, but also spouse abusers, recreational drug users, drunken and reckless drivers, illegal gamblers, and those soliciting prostitutes. The bad guys are a fairly large segment of the population.

Notwithstanding the New Hampshire police killings and despite the warlike analogies of modern police work, the number of law enforcement officers slain in the line of duty has actually been trending downward nationally for more than two decades—from more than 100 fatalities annually in the mid-1970s to about 70 at present. This does not mean, however, that the job of a police officer is any safer than before. On the contrary, the number of assaults against the police and the number of assaults with a gun have increased.

Most citizens understand and appreciate the vulnerability of police officers who are asked to risk their lives in the line of duty. In a crowded Littleton, New Hampshire, courtroom, dozens of irate townspeople voiced their support for the police by jeering and threatening one of the suspects in Officer Charron's murder, causing the authorities some concern about the safety of the defendant.

Such support for the police extends, of course, far beyond the borders of the Granite State. In a recent *USA Today* national poll, 7 in 10 adults said they believed their local police department was doing a good or very good job. As crime rates plummet in cities across the country, the police are enjoying a level of community support not seen since the early 1960s, before clashes with antiwar and civil rights demonstrators precipitated the rapid deterioration of police-community relations.

Besides their important peace-keeping function, the police serve a significant symbolic role. They represent our official line of defense against crime and chaos. The public depends on them to provide protection in a professional and civilized manner should trouble arise. In a sense, therefore, all citizens are victimized when police officers are slain in the line of duty.

But there is that other side. At times, the police represent forces of oppression. To some members of the black community, they are tools of a corrupt and racist white power structure. Tens of thousands of outraged demonstrators gathered on the streets of Brooklyn to protest Louima's beating and to attack the New York Police Department's long record of brutality.

Similarly, to some anti-government zealots, the police embody the unconstitutional and corrupt powers of "one world order" communism. Carl Drega, for example, the New Hampshire man who killed the two troopers and two other people, hardly regarded the police with good will or equanimity. He apparently saw himself as a victim of injustice whose personal financial hardships were a result of insensitive and corrupt, perhaps even evil, public officials, for whom the police were an extension.

From the most congested big city neighborhoods to the tiniest villages of New England, there is at times a vicious cycle of violence perpetrated by and against the police. Police brutality inspires some residents to get even with the "enemy." Assaults against police officers, in turn, can create a siege mentality on the part of the police, causing some of them to respond with excessive force. Both the police and aggrieved residents of the community believe they are at war with one another. In some instances, their belief helps inspire a much-too-violent reality.

Perhaps the most effective long-term strategy for reversing the vicious cycle of violence by and against the police has already been tested in our own back yard. Boston—its police and its citizenry—has been held up as a national model in reducing crime. The local rate is at a 29-year low, owing in part to increased cooperation, rather than confrontation, between the police and the public. Unlike New York, where the crime rate has come down at the expense of positive community relations, Boston's record of citizen complaints against the police—from impolite behavior to excessive force—has improved. The number of such complaints dropped from 248 in 1995 to 231 last year.

The emphasis that Police Commissioner Paul Evans has placed on professional ethics and the appropriate use of force appears to be paying off. In partnership with the community, Boston's form of neighborhood policing has been effective as a strategy to achieve peace, and not war.

Effective Police Departments Not Built Solely on Test Scores

This essay was published by Jack Levin in the Boston Herald *(September 24, 1995) following the controversial and racially charged trial of O. J. Simpson. It makes a case for assigning teams of black and white police officers to patrol inner city neighborhoods.*

In the trial of O. J. Simpson, what would have happened to the charge of police racism and coverup had black street cops and criminalists been called to testify on behalf of the prosecution?

Americans who oppose efforts to hire more black police officers have argued that race is totally irrelevant as a criterion for evaluating the adequacy of a public servant. They suggest that the job should always go to the most qualified man or woman—for example, to the candidate who scores highest on the police exam.

In light of police Detective Mark Fuhrman's role in the O. J. Simpson trial, however, the notion of "adequacy" seems ridiculously narrow when applied to "our men and women in blue." The criteria for assessing adequacy might reasonably be broadened to include the premise that black police officers can be much more effective than their white counterparts.

According to the 1968 *Report of the National Advisory Commission on Civil Disorders,* most of the riots of the 1960s in major cities were triggered by confrontations between black residents and white police officers. Moreover, there have been dozens of civil disturbances in our major cities since 1980, most of which were precipitated by clashes between a white police officer and black residents.

Any effort to reduce civil disturbances will require a long-term response aimed at giving impoverished black Americans a real sense of hope for the future. Meanwhile, we can more easily seek to postpone crises by reducing the perception that the police force is an occupying army, an armed agency of a racist white power structure.

Sociologist Alexander Thomas and I recently conducted research strongly suggesting that people's perceptions of police brutality and corruption depend on the racial identity of the police officers. We discovered that the charge of police racism is defused when a black officer is present at the scene of a confrontation—no matter what his test scores. In fact, we were unable to locate a single case of rioting in any major city that has ever been triggered by a dispute involving black police and black residents.

Wherever racial tensions run high and civil disturbances are likely to occur, police-community relations will be severely strained if exclusively white police are stationed in inner-city neighborhoods. Perhaps in part because of the pervasive national attention given to the Rodney King beating, many people have come to assume brutality and illegality on the part of white officers who arrest a black suspect, even if the arrest is conducted "by the book." In the interest of averting disaster, therefore, teams of white police officers operating in inner-city neighborhoods should never be put in a position of having to arrest a black suspect.

On the other hand, the assignment of black officers exclusively to black communities and white police exclusively to predominantly white communities is legally and morally unacceptable. It would, for one thing, create a racially segregated police force. For another, it would assure the continuing perception that wealthy and middle-income black residents are the recipients of unjust and discriminatory treatment.

Police-community tensions can be effectively reduced without segregating the force by assigning teams of white and black officers to ride together, walk their beats together and conduct arrests together. Fortunately, as a result of affirmative action guidelines, a growing number of police forces around the country have recently increased their hiring of black officers.

Get Smart—Not Tough— on Juvenile Crime

A version of this essay published by James Alan Fox and Jennifer M. Balboni in the Boston Sunday Globe *(July 2, 2000) reacts to legislative action in the U.S. Congress to toughen juvenile offender laws. It argues that trying juveniles as adults, although appropriate in certain cases, often does more harm than good.*

The recent shooting death of a popular Florida school teacher allegedly at the hands of his 13-year-old student has once again stirred debate about how best to respond to juvenile violent crime. Echoing widespread public sentiment, the posture in the political arena has been decidedly punitive, with relatively little attention to rehabilitation and treatment.

Typical of sound-bite crime control rhetoric, Alabama Governor Don Siegelman suggested that "adult crime should equal adult time." His state and most others around the nation have significantly increased the flow of juvenile offenders into adult courts and prisons.

Nearly 30,000 juvenile offenders are prosecuted in adult courts annually, more than twice as many as 15 years ago. As a consequence, the number of offenders under age 18 sentenced to serve time in an adult correctional facility has climbed, from 3,400 in 1985 to 7,400 in 1997. And it's not just the young killers and rapists who are seeing the inside of adult prison walls: Nearly a third were sentenced for non-violent offenses.

At the federal level, the Violent and Repeat Juvenile Offender Accountability and Rehabilitation Act of 1999, which currently awaits final action in Congress, proposes to expand this same hard-line approach for handling young criminals. Not only does the bill mandate adult prosecution for the few juveniles—just hundreds annually—who fall under federal jurisdiction, but it offers financial incentives for states to follow suit.

Despite the appeal of "get tough" measures like this, it is far better that we "get smart" in responding to juvenile violence. The research evidence related to the transfer of youngsters to the adult court clearly shows that adult time for juveniles often equals more crime.

THE IMPACT OF TRANSFER LAWS

Criminologist Donna Bishop and her colleagues in Florida undertook an extensive project tracking comparable groups of juveniles—some transferred to adult court and others who remained in the juvenile justice system. These researchers found that the young offenders who were transferred into the adult system recidivated both more frequently and more seriously than their counterparts who were retained by the juvenile court.

Instead of reforming or scaring juvenile offenders into becoming law-abiding citizens, adult punishments may actually increase their propensity for criminal behavior. Mixing impressionable young offenders among hardened criminals makes the wrong kind of impression upon them. If adult prisons aren't schools for crime, then at least they're study halls.

Research on the deterrent effects of juvenile transfer procedures, like those proposed in the pending federal legislation, also suggests that this may not be the smartest approach in terms of dissuading other potential offenders. Criminologists Simon Singer and David McDowall, for example, evaluated whether the landmark and widely-publicized New York Juvenile Offender Law of 1978, which prescribed adult prosecution for violent offenders as young as 14 (and 13 for murder), had any impact on juvenile crime rates. By comparing trends over time both in New York City and Philadelphia, they found that the threat promised by the tough New York statute had no effect on lowering rates of serious juvenile offending.

In a similar study, social scientists Eric Jensen and Linda Metsger compared rates of juvenile violent crime before and after the Idaho juvenile transfer law was enacted, and determined that the procedure failed to reduce the rate of violent juvenile crime. To the contrary, rates of serious juvenile violence rose in Idaho after the transfer law was enacted, while in the two neighboring states the rates declined significantly.

There is, of course, a time and a place for transferring particular juveniles—a select few—into the jurisdiction of the adult court. As long as the juvenile court model has existed, certain repeat, violent, chronic offenders have been moved up to the adult system. Some offenders have proven through their recidivism that they are not amenable to the treatment approach offered in juvenile facilities.

These difficult decisions can and should be made by juvenile court judges through a full assessment of the youngster—his or her criminal and personal histories, not by legislators attempting to prescribe transfer criteria based on worst-case scenarios. While there are a few extreme cases of ruthless offenders who, based on their history of troublemaking, appear beyond rehabilitation, legislating around the exception is hardly a smart method of crime reduction.

The pending federal legislation, however, proposes sweeping transfer procedures, not only for hardcore juveniles, but for many lesser offenders charged with drug or property crimes. Although its title references "violent and repeat" juvenile offenders, the transfer criteria make no mention of prior records, age, or level of crime severity. In fact, violent offenders often take a backseat to drug offenders in this bill.

Finally, the method of transfer proposed is equally worrisome, by allowing the prosecutor—rather than a judge—to make the decisive call of whether or not to charge a youthful offender as an adult. This is like letting a pitcher, rather than the ump, call balls and strikes.

RESPONSIBILITY AND PUNISHABILITY

From the point of view of crime victims, of course, it matters little whether their assailant is 14 or 44. A purely retributive notion of justice would ignore an offender's age in assessing the extent of harm.

But juvenile offenders do not necessarily deserve adult-like punishment, even though they may commit an adult-like crime. The inspiration for their vicious crimes often stems from their immaturity—for example, teens committing murder in order to impress their peers or even to fulfil a dare. We must fully consider the special nature of youthful offending—even murder. Teenagers may look like adults, dress like adults, act like adults, even shoot like adults, but they reason like children.

Some recent evidence from neurological studies supports the view that juveniles have a limited capacity for understanding consequences. According to Deborah Yurgelun-Todd, director of Neuropsychology and Cognitive Neuroimaging at McLean Hospital, the frontal lobe portion of the brain, which controls the ability to think matters through fully, does not tend to develop until late adolescence or early adulthood. Indeed, it has long been true that teenagers are typically impulsive—in a sense "temporary sociopaths."

Given their limited capacity for fully appreciating the negative impact of their behavior, teenagers do not deserve equal punishment as adults, except perhaps for the most chronic offenders. Diminished capacity should mean diminished punishability, especially for non-habitual offenders.

Often these are juveniles who think little and care even less about the future, who don't expect to live past their 21st birthday. The prospect of a long-term prison sentence or even the death penalty will not dissuade them in the least.

ALTERNATIVE STRATEGIES

Statistics indicate that most youthful offenders "age out" of violent criminal activity by their early twenties. Thus, locking up juveniles for decades seems both ineffective and inefficient. As a measure designed to protect public safety, it is overkill.

For the vast majority of offenders who flirt with trouble during their impulsive and reckless youth, community-based alternatives provide appropriate life skills and education to guide them into becoming productive citizens. In addition, the "restorative" approach to justice—making the offender face the human suffering caused by his or her actions and attempt to repair the harm—has been implemented successfully in New Zealand, Australia, Canada, and, to a limited degree, in the United States.

The restorative model uses the justice system as a facilitator to force offenders, despite their developmental limitations, to understand the meaning of their crimes and the effect it has had on both the victim and the larger community. The offender's "debt" is fulfilled not through serving time (although in some cases this may be necessary for public safety), but through a tangible effort to make restitution and to improve the community. In contrast to transfer and other "get tough" approaches, restorative justice programs promote offender accountability by encouraging them to answer to the reality of their actions and make appropriate restitution.

REFORMING JUVENILE JUSTICE

In recent years, the juvenile justice system has been the whipping boy for all those who look to find blame for rising levels of youth crime. Commenting on the proposed federal legislation, Senator Orrin Hatch (R-Utah) characterized the juvenile justice system as "inadequate." We tend to agree, but not necessarily for the same reasons.

Changes brought about by the U.S. Supreme Court decisions of the past three decades, although well-intentioned, have in some respects disabled the juvenile justice system. Legal reforms have taken the juvenile court begrudgingly from its original paternalistic posture toward an adversarial model—more like the adult criminal court. Notwithstanding widespread criticism, the juvenile justice system manages to provide quality services to thousands of delinquents every year.

The juvenile court, as it celebrates its 100th anniversary, is not without redemption. Before throwing the baby out with the bath water, Congress should recognize the strengths of the juvenile justice system and invest in strategies that help change reckless delinquents into responsible adults. In the final analysis, getting smart works better than getting tough in terms of reducing juvenile crime.

John Salvi's Insanity Was Ignored

Jack Levin wrote this column for the Boston Globe *(December 9, 1996) after the suicide of John Salvi, 3rd, a deeply disturbed man who had killed two women during a shooting spree at two abortion clinics. Levin contends that the jury's guilty verdict was based more on the mythology than the facts about the insanity defense.*

Nine months into a life sentence for the 1994 murders of two receptionists at Brookline reproductive clinics, John Salvi, 3rd apparently asphyxiated himself with a plastic trash-can liner. In the days just prior to his death, he reportedly was disheveled, confused, and incoherent—pretty much the same way he was characterized while on trial. To the end, Salvi continued to espouse his belief that American Catholics were being profoundly persecuted and that large-scale powerful forces were attempting to destroy the religion he claimed to love.

The jury could have found Salvi not guilty by reason of insanity, but it chose instead to ignore his delusional thinking and to convict him of the double murder.

Americans have never trusted the insanity defense, even in response to the most bizarre and psychotic crimes. Framingham resident Richard Rosenthal was recently tried by the Commonwealth of Massachusetts for killing his wife and then impaling her heart and lungs on a stake as though she were a vampire. Rosenthal's insanity plea fell on deaf ears and he was given a life sentence without parole.

Almost everybody agrees that it is crazy to treat your wife like a vampire. But in a court of law, insanity refers not to the behavior of a defendant, only to his state of mind.

No matter how hideous your crime, if you have the capacity to appreciate the criminality of your act and if you can control yourself, then you are considered sane under the law and therefore responsible for your murderous behavior.

But there are genuine cases of insanity, where a defendant simply does not appreciate the criminality of his act or cannot control it. Jurors wouldn't hold a three-year-old killer to be guilty of murder, because we acknowledge that a young child lacks the capability for understanding the wrongfulness of his behavior. Jurors wouldn't convict a severely retarded individual for the same reason.

Yet jurors typically refuse to buy the insanity defense, no matter how compelling the evidence. They tend to feel the same way about the insanity plea that the public does—that it is too frequently used to avoid a long prison sentence. Some states have moved to eliminate the insanity plea and replace it with a "guilty but mentally ill" option in response to a widespread fear that heinous crimes committed by devious but perfectly sane defendants will somehow go unpunished—that murderers who feign insanity will someday be set free to prey once again upon innocent victims.

Actually, the insanity defense is hardly ever attempted, is hardly ever successful, and is almost never a ticket out of a lengthy sentence. Only one percent of all felony defendants plead insanity. Only one in four of them are found to be not guilty. And, those few who are determined to be not guilty spend just as much time incarcerated as their counterparts who are convicted of murder.

If Salvi had been found insane, it would have been no picnic for him. But, at least, he would have received the mental health treatment that he needed in order to remain alive.

At trial, attorneys arguing the insanity of defendants often debate whether or not they had planned a homicide. The prosecution argues that a defendant capable of planning a homicide couldn't be confused enough to be insane. In Salvi's trial, it was emphasized by the prosecuting attorney that the defendant had secured the necessary semiautomatic firepower, waited until the most propitious moment to enter the clinic, gone from crime scene to crime scene, and cleverly fled the area without being apprehended for some time. How could an insane man have been so organized, so methodical, so effective?

What gets lost in the rush to prosecute is the defendant's delusional premise. John Salvi's motivation for killing had more to do with psychopathology than with any desire to save the lives of unborn infants. He sincerely believed that he was the victim of a large-scale conspiracy to destroy Catholics, perhaps all Christians, perhaps all Caucasians. He told his parents that he had seen an evil bird in the family room of their home, that he would stay up all night guarding against the presence of evil. He claimed to have watched a friend turn into a vampire. He raved and ranted about international plots to rob Catholics of jobs, to commit genocide against white people, to destroy the Catholic Church.

Sadly, our society continues to be irrational in its thinking about the insanity defense. It is too often regarded as merely a ploy for setting free hardened criminals, rather than a legitimate defense. As a result, John Salvi's decision to take his own life became his most rational decision.

Does Salvi's Suicide Show New Insanity Plea Needed?

As a companion piece to his previous essay on Salvi, Jack Levin published this column in the Boston Herald *(December 12, 1996). It evaluates a bill filed in the Massachusetts legislature to eliminate the insanity defense and replace it with a "guilty but mentally ill" alternative.*

John Salvi's suicide while imprisoned has inspired state lawmakers to reassess the adequacy of a plea of "not guilty by reason of insanity."

Last week, Massachusetts State Sen. James Jajuga (D-Methuen) filed a bill to eliminate the current insanity defense and replace it with a new plea of "guilty but mentally ill." If passed, his legislation has two important objectives: first, to help restore public confidence in our state's criminal justice system and, second, to assure that inmates are provided with the mental health treatment they require.

Many Americans have lost confidence in the courts and prisons. A recent Gallup poll reported that only 19 percent of a national sample of adult Americans express a good deal of trust in the criminal justice system.

When considering the advisability of a "guilty but mentally ill" verdict, legislators might keep in mind the public's widespread mistrust of the courts. Many citizens view the insanity defense as just another aspect of a court system that is too soft on crime. They are concerned that a clever defendant who feigns legal insanity will subsequently be set free to prey once again upon innocent citizens.

Actually, the insanity plea is so rarely successful that it misses the large number of inmates who are mentally ill and need treatment. People tend to remember the high-profile insanity cases such as John Hinckley's attempted murder of then-President Reagan in 1980 or Lorena Bobbitt's acquittal on charges related to cutting off her husband's penis.

Yet only 1 percent of all felony defendants plead insanity; only one in four of them are found not guilty. In Massachusetts, the names of Kenneth Seguin, Richard Rosenthal and John Salvi—all defendants who unsuccessfully tried the insanity defense—attest to the tremendous difficulty of pleading insanity.

To this point, the choice for jurors in Massachusetts has been dichotomous. Defendants found not guilty by reason of insanity go to a hospital for an indefinite stay and could be later released if a judge decides they are no longer a threat. Defendants found guilty go to prison, where they may never be treated for a mental illness. Having no other alternative, jurors who believe that a defendant is truly insane may refuse to risk having him or her treated and then returned to the streets. In order to protect public safety, they are likely instead to return a guilty verdict.

In such cases, the additional plea of "guilty but mentally ill" seems like a reasonable option because it recognizes a defendant's mental health problems, but still holds him responsible for his criminal behavior. Under this verdict, a convicted defendant is never released from incarceration because of a change in his state of mind. Instead, he receives psychiatric treatment until he no longer suffers from mental disease and then serves out the remainder of his sentence behind bars.

In 1974 Michigan became the first state to adopt the defense of "guilty but mentally ill," and it has becomes a model for other states to emulate. In the meantime, 14 other states have followed Michigan's lead by adding the "guilty but mentally ill" plea; most of these states have, however, retained the "not guilty by reason of insanity" verdict as well. Because the options for jurors have been expanded rather than reduced, there has been little controversy associated with establishing the alternative of "guilty but mentally ill."

While Sen. Jajuga's bill is a significant step forward, the experience of other states suggests that the proposed legislation very much needs to be modified before it is accepted by the Massachusetts Legislature. To protect the rights of the legally insane as well as the public, Massachusetts should follow the lead of states like Michigan, Indiana, Illinois and South Dakota, where the scope of the law has been expanded to include "not guilty by reason of insanity" and "guilty but mentally ill."

There are always at least a few defendants who are genuinely unable to understand the criminality of their offenses. Some are convinced that they are killing gophers, not human beings; others hear voices commanding them to kill in order to prevent earthquakes or hurricanes. It would be an unforgivable mistake if our criminal justice system were to treat those inflicted with severe mental illnesses as indistinguishable from cunning sociopaths.

If modified to retain the insanity defense, the Jajuga bill would expand the options for jurors, increase confidence in the courts and provide much-needed treatment for our most vulnerable defendants. Reforming the court system makes good common sense, but eliminating the insanity defense should make us all feel guilty.

When Crime Pays
and Punishment Doesn't
Fit the Crime

We published this essay several years ago in the Quincy Patriot Ledger *(March 15, 1985). It demonstrates just how bizarre the plea bargaining process can become when it involves negotiating with brutal murderers.*

Whoever says that crime doesn't pay hasn't heard about Clifford R. Olson. From November 1980 to August 1981, the 42 year-old Olson beat, strangled or stabbed to death three boys and eight girls ranging in age from 9 to 18.

The Royal Canadian Mounted Police kept Olson, who lived in Vancouver, under close surveillance as their prime suspect in several unsolved disappearances of children. Olson was eventually arrested for suspicion of murder, but the evidence against him was far from strong.

Following his arrest, Olson successfully made a deal with the prosecution for his guilty plea to the murders. In return, he would receive $10,000 for each body to which he directed the police. Suspicious that investigators might renege on their promise, he demanded that $100,000 be deposited in a trust account from which the money would be paid to his wife and child while he served a life term in prison.

Prosecutors were afraid of setting a dangerous legal precedent; other criminals might see this as a way to make murder pay. But they agreed and paid Olson's wife $90,000.

The prosecutors had feared that their circumstantial evidence was less than compelling enough to convict Olson of first-degree murder. They argued that he may well have been convicted of only a single second-degree murder charge and given a paltry 10-year sentence unless they made the deal. They also rationalized that the families of the missing youngsters deserved to know whether their children were dead or alive.

The case of Clifford Olson represents an extreme and unusual version of plea bargaining. In the more common example, a defendant agrees to plead guilty after negotiating for a reduced charge or lighter sentence than he might have received had he pleaded innocent at a trial. In this way, the prosecution is spared the time and expense of a lengthy trial, and the defendant obtains a lighter sentence and/or a better chance for early parole.

Opponents of plea bargaining point out that too many felons "get off" by pleading guilty to a less serious charge. In contrast, proponents assert that the American system of justice would collapse if every case had to be tried.

But neither opponents nor proponents generally appreciate the full extent to which plea bargaining influences the disposition of serious offenses. Few, on either side of the question, refer to Olson's use of plea bargaining to secure $90,000 for his wife and child. Few cite the many other cases of informants who, in exchange for information about their confederates in crime, go free or spend little time behind bars—cases in which police can only break a code of silence by awarding one partner in crime an absurdly light punishment or no punishment at all. Whether or not justifiable, this practice assures that at least some of the offenders will be punished.

The resolution of San Francisco's infamous Zebra slayings in 1974, for instance, hinged largely on the eyewitness testimony of an informant—Anthony C. Harris—who had been paroled recently from San Quentin. As the prosecution's key witness, Harris educated the court about the six-month reign of terror in San Francisco, which resulted in the murder of 14 people.

Harris talked about the activities of a Black Muslim cult called the Death Angels. He recalled their preaching of hatred for whites, described their slayings in detail, and identified the killers by name. Testifying under a grant of immunity from prosecution, he claimed to have driven around with the defendants while they killed and maimed white "devils," but he never admitted any direct participation in the crimes.

Attorneys for the defense tried in vain to discredit Harris. They argued that he was insane and therefore unreliable; that he had perjured himself in order to hide the fact that he really was the Zebra slayer; and that he was after a $30,000 reward that the mayor of San Francisco had amassed from donations and city funds for information leading to the killers' arrest and conviction.

Whatever his motivation, Harris was ready to cooperate, but only with a promise of immunity from the "top." Homicide inspectors were more than willing to comply. In the early morning hours, Mayor Alioto personally met with Harris to assure him that he would do "whatever the law permits to be done in such cases" and "see to it that (his) wife gets the reward."

Harris then talked, but never about himself. He went completely free; each of the four defendants against whom he testified was sentenced to life in prison.

Plea bargaining may be necessary, as some argue. But negotiations with brutal murderers to obtain a guilty plea or to secure their testimony against other brutal murderers ought to be reserved as strictly a choice of last resort. Paying killers for information, risking the lives of criminals induced to turn snitches, punishing accomplices unequally, and even letting some killers go free for the sake of information, all raise difficult ethical or practical dilemmas.

As a result, these practices never should be regarded as a substitute for thorough investigation and independent gathering of facts. Nothing less than the credibility of the entire criminal justice system is at stake.

When the End Justifies
the Means

James Alan Fox contributed this column to USA Today *(June 18, 1987)
in the wake of the jury verdict in the trial of Bernhard Goetz. Despite
widespread public support for the jury's decision, Fox finds reason to be
concerned about the dangerous precedent set in the case of New York's
"subway vigilante."*

Throughout history, juries have sometimes acted on their emotions, even when contrary to the law. The jury in the Bernhard Goetz case decided that Goetz's shooting the four youths who confronted him was justified. But it seems to have justified the act because of events and issues unrelated to what transpired that day in the subway.

In acquitting Goetz of attempted murder, the jury was not reacting just to the reported gleam in Troy Canty's eye, the smile on his face, or the intrusive demand for $5. The jury, like Goetz himself, reacted as much, if not more, to the everyday mood on the subway, and in our streets as well, brought on by years of rampant crime and violence.

The jurors placed themselves In Goetz's shoes. They felt his apprehensiveness at riding the subway. They understood his unease resulting from previous muggings and applauded his refusal to be victimized anymore. The jurors, themselves fed up with crime, in the final analysis voted for at least one victim to prevail.

What's so wrong with the jury system when it imputes real emotions into the impartial structure of law? Why shouldn't the Goetz jury have tested the law of self-defense in the context of a dirty, dark, and dangerous subway car, rather than In the context of sterile law school hypotheticals?

The problem lies in deciding that the end justifies the means. Goetz's supporters point out what the youths were like—their appearance, their character, their background—and argue that Goetz's suspicions at the time were borne out in the end. "The teenagers were looking for trouble," they say, "and found it."

We should feel compassion for Goetz, but we must not justify his actions. We cannot justify an assault just because of what might have happened or because of what his victims were. This opens too many doors for other citizens to overreact when their fears, suspicions, or prejudices are aroused.

According to reports, several jurors left the courtroom Tuesday gesturing victory signs. To some people, the verdict is but "one for the good guys." It may have been a victory for Goetz and perhaps for several of the jurors, but for a society governed not by fear but by law, this is a defeat which may come back to haunt us.

Stop Sending Folks to Jail

This column was written by James Alan Fox for the Quincy Patriot
Ledger *(August 11, 1984) during a period of prison expansion. Who
would have known that the argument for selective incarceration advanced
then would be even more relevant today with nearly two million
Americans behind bars?*

While a maturing U.S. population has, as expected, produced a three-year drop in the national crime rate, the size of our prison population keeps setting new records each year. Unlike the crime boom of last decade, which society accepted and combated the best it could, our ability to cope with burgeoning inmate counts is restricted by the limited availability of jail space.

Nationally, our prisons are oversubscribed by between two percent and 18 percent, depending on how one defines capacity; In Massachusetts, matters are far worse with a prison population 47 percent over our prison capacity.

An underlying reason is the vastly changing correctional philosophy sweeping this country. Discouragement over the crime wave of the 1960s and 1970s, mixed with a general conservative swing, has pressured legislatures and courts to opt for more punishment: mandatory minimum sentences, longer sentences, determinant sentences, and the decreased use of parole.

That trend has wiped out—or at least dampened—another trend that would have reduced the need for prison beds in the late 1980s: the shift in the nation's age structure out of the prison-prone younger years.

The problem over prison crowding is more than an issue of numbers and figures, and more than the issue of discomfort for inmates doubled and tripled up in cells. Seven states have had their correctional systems declared unconstitutional in violation of the Eighth Amendment against "cruel and unusual" punishment. Many others have been compelled by court order to reduce prison populations. More states may be forced to adopt procedures like Michigan's automatic reductions in prison terms under "emergency" conditions of crowding, or Minnesota's sentencing guidelines that are linked to prison space availability.

So what should be done? Rather than boosting capacity through new construction at a hefty cost of over $50,000 per prison bed, we ought to make less use of imprisonment as a form of punishment.

The objective of deterrence, rooted in mandatory sentencing for offenses from gun possession to drug sales, also can be achieved through noncustodial penalties. Only 38 percent of our nation's prisoners are incarcerated for violent crimes, down from 50 percent of years ago.

Many prisoners can be released to community settings, safely and at a lower correctional cost, where they can perform needed community service and work to pay restitution to their victims. This would make room for those who truly need to be kept securely away from us.

Unless we seriously consider a move to deinstitutionalize, any decision to build more prisons will prove fruitless. By the turn of the century, prison space needs will reach unprecedented levels, following a 1990s mini crime wave brought on by the young offspring of the baby boomers, the so-called "baby boomerang" effect.

By that time, we may have to resort to outer space to solve the problem of prison space. Like the prison ships used by the British in the 18th century (and proposed here periodically, using old Navy vessels), correctional spaceships and sheriffs shuttles may be our future vehicles for short-term confinement. Like the famous prison colonies once used by England and France, lunar colonies may in the future provide secure facilities for society's outcasts.

In the meantime, we should make do with the facilities we have wherever possible, aside from, of course, the remodeling and upgrading that many of them sorely require.

PART **X**

■ ■ ■ ■ ■ ▬▬▬▬▬▬▬▬▬▬▬▬▬▬▬▬▬▬▬▬▬▬▬▬▬▬▬▬▬

CAPITAL PUNISHMENT

■ ■ ■ ■ ■ ▬▬▬▬▬▬▬▬▬▬▬▬▬▬▬▬▬▬▬▬▬▬▬▬▬▬▬▬▬

Life without Hope

In this essay, which was published in the Boston Herald *(November 24, 1991), James Alan Fox presents a beefed-up alternative to the death penalty.*

The ink is barely dry on Gov. William Weld's proposal to the Legislature for the reinstatement of the death penalty in Massachusetts, and debate has already started in full force. While it may be a long time until this issue is settled—Rep. James Brett, chairman of the Committee of Criminal Justice has basically declared it dead on arrival for this session—and even longer until we witness an execution in the Commonwealth, there will certainly be no lack of excitement in the meantime.

Despite the enthusiasm and passion on both sides, there is actually little that will distinguish this debate from the hundreds that we have heard before. We will again have heated dialogue about morality, sprinkled with choice references to the scriptures in support of both sides of the death penalty question. Criminologists will undoubtedly point out the dearth of solid statistical evidence of a deterrent effect; others will respond that death remains the ultimate threat and that we need to make the death penalty a realistic threat—swift and sure.

We will also be presented with elaborate cost assessments of the money needed to house and feed convicted killers and with the counter argument that the legal machinery associated with prosecuting a death penalty case is perhaps just too expensive. And if all else fails, abolitionists will quote the statistics on wrongful executions, while death-penalty advocates will downplay

117

the risks of mistake in light of the innocent victims potentially saved because of the death penalty. There will be plenty about which to argue.

Interestingly, there is one point on which we all can agree, and thus a point from which we should start to fashion change. At least some killers have committed crimes so perverse, so grotesque, and so atrocious that they should never walk out of prison no matter what.

Most informed citizens are aware, of course, that Massachusetts law does indeed mandate life imprisonment without parole eligibility for all persons convicted of first-degree murder. But everyone knows that life imprisonment does not often mean life in prison. Parole ineligibility does not mean that a lifer cannot be paroled, that is, once he is made parole-eligible through a commutation to second-degree murder. With very good reason and many examples to cite, citizens fear that somehow, someday, be it through furlough, commutation, or good-time credit, lifers will be released by our criminal justice system, perhaps when we're not looking.

More than just posing a threat to the safety of our neighborhoods, maneuvers to circumvent parole ineligibility of first-degree murderers breed skepticism and distrust among the citizens toward the entire system of justice. In response, death-penalty advocates exploit this fear and distrust by suggesting that an execution is the only sure-fire way of preventing a killer from repeating his crime some day in the future.

But if the principal concern rests with how the criminal justice system deals with murderers once they are sentenced, then we should attack this issue directly. If we're worried that murderers will escape, then put them on an island. If we're concerned about parole or commutation, then work to change these provisions. It surely seems to be overkill to execute a convict in order to prevent him from ever being let out of prison alive.

As an alternative to Weld's death-penalty bill therefore, I would like to propose a new penalty, "life without hope." Certain killers should be sentenced to life without parole eligibility, without commutation eligibility, without good-time credit eligibility, without furlough eligibility, and without the slightest shred of hope.

In designing a "life without hope" bill, we will of course, need to distinguish among different kinds of killers, to separate the bad guys from the really bad guys.

A further implication of this idea is the abolition of the mandatory life imprisonment without parole eligibility, at least as we know it. Rather, first-degree murderers shall receive "life without hope" if aggravating circumstances are found, yet "life with parole eligibility" if mitigating circumstances are present. The concept of truth in sentencing applies both ways.

There are ample opinion polls to suggest that the notion of life without hope could garner widespread support. Although three-quarters of citizens favor the death penalty—regardless of race, sex, political party, when asked if they prefer capital punishment over life imprisonment (as opposed to a life sentence), the death penalty loses out every time.

No one wants to see our most vicious criminals—serial murderers and child killers—get paroled in a matter of a few years. If this were the case, die-hard opponents of capital punishment, like myself, might change our stand. But a guarantee that brutal killers will be kept behind bars where they belong is something that we can all live with.

After all is said and done, the death penalty is still an important symbol to some people. In putting forth his new bill, Gov. Weld commented that he wants to express his intolerance for murder by reinstating the death penalty. Well, Governor, we are all intolerant when it comes to murder, but some of us don't have to kill to prove it.

Is the Death Sentence Justice or Vengeance?

In this essay, published in the Cleveland Plain Dealer *(May 18, 1994),*
James Alan Fox comments on the celebratory mood surrounding the
execution of serial killer John Wayne Gacy.

Hearing the news bulletin that serial killer John Wayne Gacy had indeed been executed saddened me greatly. It is not that I will miss Gacy in any way or that I feel at all sorry for him. My sadness is that so many Americans are happy about his execution.

In days surrounding Gacy's execution, the good people of Illinois celebrated a disgraceful orgy of vengeance. There was dancing in the streets of Chicago. Some celebrants wore party hats and others dressed in clown suits, reminiscent of the cheerful character that Gacy assumed to entertain children. One local radio personality even organized a Gacy Day Parade, with "Hello Gacy" as the theme song arranged to the tune of "Hello Dolly."

Outside the Stateville Correctional Center where the execution was performed, the revelry was especially intense. Death penalty supporters cheered and held signs that read "Gacy—stick it to him" and "Goodbye Gacy. It's time for you to fry." (Actually, with Illinois' use of lethal injection, the only thing to fry was the chicken dinner that Gacy ordered as his last meal.)

As is customary at most executions these days, the pro-capital punishment party-goers were joined by some anti-capital punishment party-poopers. The small group of abolitionists were, however, no match for those who found vengeance something in which to rejoice. Death penalty advocates have clearly won over the majority of Americans, and those few of us opponents who are left are easily dismissed with disdain along with the ACLU.

The difficulty with trying to defend the anti-death penalty position is that supporters can concede most of the points yet simply appeal to the desire for revenge. How can you argue with someone who insists on vengeance against infamous killers like John Gacy, Ted Bundy or Charles Manson? We may be the only civilized society that has not abolished capital punishment, but then we are also the only society plagued by serial killers.

If anything positive comes from Gacy's execution, perhaps it may assuage the public's overwhelming thirst for vengeance. If we give death penalty enthusiasts a "big one" like Gacy, maybe they will be less vehement in demanding the execution of hundreds of lesser-known condemned murderers whose death sentences were more a spillover reaction to infamous serial killers like Gacy than to the specific details of their own crimes. Unfortunately, I tend to doubt that my hopes will be realized. When you throw a pack of lions a huge steak, they only get more bloodthirsty.

While death penalty supporters cling to the revenge motive as if it were an inalienable right of citizenship guaranteed by the Constitution, the so-called "an eye for an eye, tooth for a tooth" logic for capital punishment actually crumbles upon close scrutiny. Our system of justice does not operate on the notion of punishing offenders in the same way that they punished their victims. We do not rape rapists or steal the cars of auto thieves, so why must we kill killers?

In a civilized society, we use imprisonment as the means for expressing our intolerance for criminality. The more severe the crime, the longer the term of incarceration. Gacy and other serial killers forfeit their right ever to live free, but not their right to live. For them, life without parole is the civilized punishment.

I have even heard it said in recent days that capital punishment is too good for John Gacy, that he should have suffered the same kind of horrible death that he inflicted on his victims. Aside from the fact that anyone who makes such a statement does not fully understand the horror of an execution, capital punishment is in a sense more brutal and reprehensible than any of the murders committed by Gacy or others of his kind.

In my years studying serial killers, I have encountered the most vile and most despicable acts of inhumanity. Yet, I have never known a serial killer to cage his victims, tell them precisely when they were going to die, let them wait years for their destiny, and then audaciously ask what they might favor for their last meal.

Unlike the scores of executions that have been carried out in recent years without much fanfare or media hype, the publicity surrounding Gacy's execution, particularly during the final countdown to the wee hours of May 10th, affected most of us in some way or another. Next time, if you can't spare the life of the condemned, then at least spare us from having to watch a most shameful aspect of our American culture—the celebration of vengeance.

A Freeze on Executions

This essay, which we published in the Boston Herald *(October 5, 1992), takes a somewhat tongue-in-cheek look at the fallibility of the death penalty.*

Criminologist Richard Moran of Mt. Holyoke College may have been facetious when he suggested cryogenics—the process of deep freezing the terminally ill—as an alternative to capital punishment for convicted murderers. "Let's freeze them until we find the cure for crime," Moran quipped.

Actually, Professor, your concept of "just-ice" may not be such a bad idea after all for dealing with cold-blooded killers. Freezing is obviously cleaner and more humane than present-day methods such as the electric chair or even lethal injections. Let us not forget when "Old Sparky" malfunctioned during a Florida execution or the suffering caused by so-called "painless" injections of lethal drugs. More important, if it turns out that the condemned was in fact innocent, we can always defrost him.

The risk of error in the application of the death penalty is far from trivial, according to a detailed investigation by Hugo Bedau of Tufts University and Michael Radelet of the University of Florida. Bedau and Radelet identified 350 innocent persons who were wrongly convicted of capital crimes in the United States since 1900. One-hundred-thirteen of these miserable souls had been condemned to die for their crimes. Happily, most of these men and women were saved from an unjust execution, when new evidence was uncovered or the real culprit confessed. Twenty-two of these lucky ones were exonerated within hours before they were to be executed, and one William Mason Wellman was already strapped into the electric chair when the real perpetrator came forward to confess. Another twenty-three were not so fortunate, however; their vindication came posthumously.

Regrettably, there is little to indicate that we have more safeguards in place today. A recent survey of persons sentenced to death between 1987 and 1989 uncovered twelve cases in which the convict was completely cleared "before it was too late." Moreover, the recent trend by the U.S. Supreme Court and in Congress to curtail the appeals process will likely increase the risk of an improper execution.

Obviously, we are not *really* suggesting that we replace death row with a big ice cube tray. The notion of putting killers "on ice" is only figurative. A life sentence can be a viable alternative to the death penalty, because it is reversible should the convict later prove to be innocent.

Of course, the reversibility of a life sentence is also the major reason why so many citizens oppose it. Everyone knows that life imprisonment does not often mean life in prison. In some states, lifers can be paroled; in other states that have "life without parole" laws, sentences may still be commuted by the governor. As a result, Americans have absolutely no confidence in the criminal justice system and insist on the death penalty as the only sure-fire way to protect society.

If we're concerned murderers will escape, then put them on an island. If we're worried about parole or commutation, then work to change the law. It surely seems to be overkill to execute a convict in order to prevent him from ever leaving prison alive.

A life sentence should be reversible, but only if the prisoner is later found to be innocent—*not* if he is deemed rehabilitated, *not* if he later shows remorse, *not* even if he becomes terminally ill. Being humane simply does not require being lenient or soft. We don't have to freeze convicted murderers—just make sure not to free them from the "cooler."

The Senate's Empty Gesture

In this essay, which was published in the Palm Beach Post *(June 5, 1990), we question the sense behind the U.S. Senate debate over executing the mentally retarded.*

Good news for abolitionists: It may soon be illegal to execute retarded spies. Following heated debate, the United States Senate, by a wide margin of 59 to 38, moved to bar the federal government from executing offenders with low IQs.

Voting against the measure, Senator Orrin Hatch, Republican of Utah, argued passionately that this exclusion would create a loophole which would open the floodgates. He voiced concern that every defendant facing the death penalty would claim to be retarded.

Hatch has a great sense of humor, even if he's not joking. Following his logic, our federal justice system would be thrown into chaos. The insanity defense would soon be supplanted by the stupidity defense; the lie detector test would be replaced by the IQ test. Future Julius and Ethel Rosenbergs would plead, "we're not Communists, just dumb."

Now that the retardation exclusion is likely to become federal law, people like Senator Hatch will be looking for a foolproof test to identify those defendants who are clever enough to look retarded. As always, to be criminally responsible, you must know right from wrong; but now to be eligible for the death penalty, you must know right from left!

As for those senators in the majority who supported the ban, their vote may appear to be a courageous move, if not an act of political suicide. Poll after poll suggest a pervasive pro-death penalty mood in America. In response to the public mandate, there has been a strong resurgence of executions in this country. The United States Supreme Court, furthermore, has confirmed the constitutionality of executing those with substandard intelligence. In the High Court's view, it is simply not cruel and unusual punishment.

Upon closer examination, however, the Senate was more cowardly than courageous. After striking down more controversial and important amendments concerning racial discrimination and appellate review in death penalty cases, the senators took an easy stand that they must have known would not have been unpopular with their constituents. Last year's *Time* magazine national poll showed that only 30 percent of Americans favors executing the retarded.

More than just politically expedient, the Senate ban is an empty gesture. Most violent crimes fall under state jurisdiction. For example, a convicted killer with a borderline IQ was recently executed in Louisiana, when the Governor ignored the recommendation of his Board of Pardons to commute the sentence to life. In Louisiana, like most states that have capital punishment statutes, mental retardation does not preclude the death penalty.

The federal criminal code, in contrast, has very limited jurisdiction. Since 1930, therefore, only 33 of the approximately 4,000 executions in the United States were carried out under federal authority; and these few often involved offenses requiring at least normal intelligence, such as espionage and sabotage, or even kidnapping. It is doubtful that any of these few federal executions would have fallen under the purview of the Senate prohibition.

Perhaps the Senate action has some symbolic meaning for abolitionists. If passed by the House and signed into law by the President, it might even encourage state lawmakers across the country to follow suit. In the meantime, however, the federal ban on executing the retarded won't amount to a Capitol Hill of beans.

Too Easy to Kill

James Alan Fox prepared this eyewitness account of a Missouri execution for the Boston Globe *(December 29, 1996). He argues that the move to reduce the brutality of the death penalty may have had an unintended consequence.*

I have long been a vocal opponent of capital punishment, publishing my share of academic studies and testifying before legislative bodies on a few occasions. Despite all my reading, research, and reflection on the evils of execution, I had never witnessed one first-hand…that is, not until last night.

I flew from Providence to Potosi, Missouri, a small "prison town" two hours south of St. Louis, to serve as a state's witness to the execution of Richard Zeitvogel. A 40-year-old career criminal, Zeitvogel had cold-bloodedly murdered two cell mates while incarcerated for the 1976 rape and robbery of a Pulaski County family. In the crime that earned him the time, Zeitvogel had forced the terrified homeowner to watch as he and his buddies raped the man's wife in the spirit of camaraderie.

Now I would be the one to do the watching, as the State of Missouri would take Zeitvogel's life by means of lethal injection. Of course, I was not forced to witness this act of violence, and my willingness, though conveniently couched in terms of scholarly curiosity, made me feel self-conscious about my somewhat voyeuristic voyage to the "Show Me" state.

My qualms were further reinforced by friends and family who urged me to pass on the midnight madness, arguing that it was morally wrong even to participate in the process. Up to the very last minute, my wife appealed to me by telephone to forgo the last leg of my expedition and to stay at the motel for the night. There would be no staying tonight, neither for me nor for the execution.

The condemned convict hardly attracted much sympathy or support. After all, this was a man whose tattooed chest displayed the inscription, "Beat me, execute me, but warden don't bore me." Protesters outside the prison, if there were any, were hard to find, even in the flood of high intensity light illuminating the 800-bed institution under a tight execution-eve lock-down.

Arriving at the prison before 10:30 P.M. for the pre-execution routine, I began to get nervous. I passed some time chatting with the commissioner and her staff about current trends in correctional research. We avoided the subject of the death penalty. They knew of my opposition, and killing was their duty. It was neither the time nor the place for a debate.

Meanwhile, Richard Zeitvogel, the center of attention, was busy with his own preparations. He spent the day meeting with visiting family members. He then enjoyed a final feast consisting of a T-bone streak, a burger, fried shrimp and fried mushrooms, washed down by a cold chocolate shake. For dessert, Zeitvogel received two doses of sedative.

As midnight approached, the other witnesses and I were ushered into a viewing gallery, furnished with two rows of chairs and protected by a partition with ample glass windows into the execution chamber. Venetian blinds were drawn over the windows to protect the anonymity of the executioner as he made final preparations. Still, we could hear him doing the death work.

On command, at the stroke of midnight, the blinds were raised, revealing the simple execution apparatus. Covered to his neck in a white sheet, Zeitvogel was resting on a gurney with an intravenous tube running from his arm through a small hole in the wall behind his head. Whether it was the sedative or his own disregard for life, Zeitvogel seemed to be the calmest participant in the whole process. He showed no signs of struggle or distress. He just lay quietly, looking at his family through the glass as they waved their goodbyes.

The warden yelled out the commands for each stage of the "operation," as it was called. At 12:02 A.M., sodium pentothal was passed through Zeitvogel's intravenous, rendering him unconscious. A minute later, the warden gave the order for stage two; pancronium bromide was injected to halt Zeitvogel's breathing, although the change was hardly noticeable. At the next command, potassium chloride was passed through the IV tube, stopping the convict's heart function. At 12:05 P.M., the warden announced, "operation completed," and Richard Zeitvogel was pronounced dead. The entire process had taken just three unspectacular minutes.

The execution itself was far less than I had expected, quite underwhelming. The State of Missouri had completely removed all the horror from the process—no smoking fleshing from Ol' Sparky and no frantic struggle for air in the gas chamber.

Lethal injection is designed to take the barbarism out of the death penalty. In my mind, it had the opposite effect. It was so straight-forward and sterile that it was just too easy. It should not be that easy to take human life. It should be agonizing—not for the condemned but for the rest of us.

In the end, according to a prepared statement from the governor which was read aloud at the post-execution press conference, justice had been served. Zeitvogel had killed two inmates, and the State of Missouri had killed one.

■ ■ ■ ■ ■

PART XI

VICTIMS

■ ■ ■ ■ ■

San Ysidro's Shameful Apathy

James Alan Fox wrote this essay for the San Diego Union *(February 19, 1986), inspired by his visit to the scene of the July 1984 mass murder at a McDonald's restaurant in San Ysidro, California. He reflects on the failure of local residents and community leaders to memorialize the site in an appropriate way. Eventually, the city did build a fitting and tasteful monument to the victims.*

Having studied the phenomenon of mass murder for five years, I have become pretty good at distancing myself emotionally from this horrible topic. Friends and colleagues alike often ask me how I can stand it, all the gore, all the viciousness, all the violence. Except for an occasional nightmare about bodies buried underneath my house, it really doesn't bother me anymore. I've gotten used to it.

And so, during a convention of criminologists in San Diego, I seized the opportunity to visit nearby San Ysidro, the site of the tragic mass murder at a McDonald's restaurant two summers ago in which 21 died and another 19 were wounded.

I recall the face of James Huberty, the killer. His bespectacled profile was shown everywhere in the media. But I can't quite recollect the names of the victims, and I don't even remember seeing their pictures. It is a shame that America remembers the names Huberty, Whitman, and Speck—all of whom have committed horrible massacres—yet few recall any of their victims' names, besides those who knew them personally.

Upon reaching San Ysidro, I wasn't really sure what to look for. I thought I had read about a plan to erect a playground and memorial on the site, but I saw no trace of either. I stopped at a roadside motel to ask for directions. The clerk, annoyed by my irreverent pursuit, curtly directed me to a vacant dirt lot next to a donut shop.

I drove into the lot, but there was no sign amidst the darkness of night that anything had ever happened here. But then as I turned the car around to leave, the headlights illuminated a blue, wooden shed.

It was a shrine—not a cold and impersonal marble monument, but an impoverished, yet genuine, tribute to the neighborhood children who were tragically and violently slain. Inside the shrine hung paintings of Jesus and the Virgin Mary, adorned with candles and fresh flowers. Vandals had tried to deface the shrine by smashing its figurines and by spraying it with paint.

But still visible were the names and ages of the victims, which had been written with a marker along the walls. I paused at the name of Carlos Reyes, Jr., 8 months old, as I thought about my own child safe back in Boston. But then several mothers and fathers probably thought their children were safe, too, that summer day in sending them to McDonald's for a burger.

I stared at the names of the victims, names I had never before bothered to read closely, let alone commit to memory. The shrine wasn't at all what I had expected, nor did I expect it would affect me as deeply as it did. I had always understood intellectually the sorrowful aftermath of a mass murder, but I never let it touch me personally. There was something about this crude, handmade memorial that got through to me. I wept.

After returning to Boston, I felt compelled to investigate further the background of the shrine in San Ysidro. I learned of an ancient Mexican custom, observed primarily in the interior of that country, by which the spot where someone dies is sacred; it is held that the spirit of the deceased remains there.

I discovered that many residents opposed the shrine; they wanted to tear down what they felt was an eyesore, particularly those in San Ysidro who saw this dreadful mass murder as a dubious claim to national recognition.

"Why enshrine this spot?" they contended. It's not a battlefield where heroes sacrificed their lives in defense of their country. Rather, the McDonald's massacre is something that most would like to forget. The proper place for the parents to pay their respects, to lay their flowers, and say their prayers are the gravesites where the bodies are buried.

Opponents to the San Ysidro shrine argued that this is America, and that ancestral customs must not interfere with the American way of life. Indeed, this obtrusive religious symbol was very much out of place among the gas stations and fast-food restaurants that surrounded it on commercialized San Ysidro Boulevard.

Sadly, the official position of the City of San Diego stands also in opposition to the shrine: The land, given to the city by the McDonald's Corporation, is now public property and so religious symbols are deemed inappropriate. I had hoped that Tom Arena, the man who built and maintained the shrine, would persevere against the tremendous resistance to his tribute.

Last month, I learned that Mr. Arena had finally succumbed to the many forces against him, leaving the shrine for vandals to scavenge. I'm sorry it had to end this way. I keep feeling that the poor victims of this tragedy—both those who died and those who mourn—have been twice victimized.

Twenty-one young lives were taken by the killer's bullets. Even more shameful—simply because it is so unnecessary—is the intolerance of an apathetic community, disrespectful street vandals, and an unfeeling city government to the observance of old-world customs when they begin to interfere with "progress."

A Train Tragedy Humanized

James Alan Fox wrote this first person account of the aftermath of a
human tragedy. In the Boston Herald *(June 8, 2000), he reports how*
easy it is for bystanders to distance themselves from death—especially
when they don't have to confront it.

Fortunate that my Monday agenda ended early, I ran to catch the 12:13 P.M. commuter train home from Ruggles Street Station. I was to meet up with my 15-year-old son after school and spend some quality time on the baseball field. Instead, I spent the afternoon focused on another boy—a boy whose death was just a few minutes and a few miles down the track.

Shortly after the train pulled away from Canton Junction, I heard the shrill blast of the whistle followed by the agonizing screech of the brakes— the awful sound of metal upon metal.

"What now?" I wondered with a bit of impatience and annoyance as the train came to a halt. "Another MBTA screw-up?"

The conductor—a woman who showed little emotion—passed through the train to announce that there had been a fatality. The train had struck a pedestrian.

"That's too bad," passengers responded, "How long do you think we'll be stuck here?"

Whatever air of concern there was at first quickly changed into a collective sense of irritation. Several passengers were concerned about missing appointments. One older woman worried out loud about how she would retrieve her grandchildren after school.

Death can be tragic but lives go on. One man questioned why the train couldn't just back up and then switch over to the other track. Apparently, the body lay beneath the train, preventing us from moving until the evidence was removed by the medical examiner.

"It would take awhile," we were informed.

No one was permitted to leave the train. Yet a few indignant passengers refused to be held hostage by the MBTA and jumped off anyway.

After well over an hour, we were advised that we could wait for several hours more until the scene was cleared and the train could proceed, or we could be shepherded back to Canton Junction. But there was a catch: We would have to walk past the body.

As several passengers quietly weighed their options, police and fire-fighters gathered alongside the train, inspecting the grim scene and taking their measurements.

Being in the business of studying murder, my own exasperation was eclipsed by curiosity. I maneuvered my way through the cars toward the rear of the train, despite the woman conductor's admonition to stay up front.

The rear car was dark and empty except for a couple of MBTA employees. I walked to the window at the back and gazed down at the tracks. Between the rails just behind the train lay the body shrouded with a small white sheet that managed not to cover nearly enough of it. A pair of sneakers were strewn on the tracks. They appeared to be the kind that boys wear—boys about my son's age.

In my profession, I have dealt with violent death before. Yet the contrast between the eerie stillness of the scene before me and the impatient chatter of passengers up front made me ill.

An announcement came over the speaker that a bus would soon arrive to take us to our destinations. We were led away from the train, not near the body after all but through a neighboring yard. TV camera crews filmed our exodus as if we were something more than inconsequential bystanders—as if we, too, were victims.

Once aboard the bus, several commuters complained about the slow response time until our evacuation and the circuitous route the bus was following. They seemed to have forgotten why we had been detained. It is not that they were callous people. Rather they were detached from the tragedy by the span of several train cars, and were able to disassociate their inconvenience from the death of a boy.

I have not been able to shake the image of those remains on the track and of the boy's sneakers. His name was Matthew Melket and he was only 17 and a student at Canton High School.

Friends have asked why I would have wanted to look at that grim scene. I'm not sorry I did. Seeing is much more than believing; it humanizes tragedy.